God's
Garden

God's
Garden

Children's Stories Grown
from the Bible

By Adam Fisher

BEHRMAN HOUSE, INC.

For Liana Rose and Michaela Eve,

two of the precious jewels in my story,

with love from Grandpa.

May they add their own stories to these.

Library of Congress Cataloging–in–Publication Data

Fisher, Adam, 1941-
     God's garden: children's stories grown from the Bible/by Adam Fisher
        p.   cm.
     Summary: Each of forty-six original stories based upon events in
     the five books of Moses is followed by a lesson to dramatize its
     contemporary significance.
     ISBN 0-87441-696-5
     1. Bible stories, English--O.T. Pentateuch.
     [1. Bible stories--O.T. Pentateuch.] I. Title.
     BS551. 2. F499   1999
     222'. 109505—dc21   99-32339
                                           CIP

Manufactured in the United States of America

TABLE OF CONTENTS

Leviticus

Numbers

Deuteronomy

INTRODUCTION

For the past 30 years I have been telling stories to children, mostly at Family Shabbat Services. I have seen firsthand the power of stories to engage the mind and heart, to delight, to teach, and most of all, to engross children and adults in the Bible. This type of storytelling is a process—a process of living with and in a text, of asking questions and imagining answers. What happened to Joseph on his way into Egypt? What did Moses experience as he was growing up that prepared him to have such a sense of moral outrage that he killed an Egyptian who was beating an Israelite? For Jews, this process is called Torah. Torah is more than a book; it is also the process of engaging the Book. The richest Jewish expression of this process is found in the classical midrash, whose basic method is used in many of these stories. Many of the stories in this book are entirely original works, while others contain elements from classical tales, Midrash, and commentaries.

Parallels to this approach can be found in other traditions. For example, the Patristic literature of early Christianity, as well as many modern pastors in their sermons and homilies, use these same techniques to elucidate or contemporize the meaning of ancient texts.

God's Garden is designed for use by people of all faiths. Rabbis, ministers, teachers, camp counselors, and of course parents will find stories to teach values and engage the imagination of children. Each story is related to a biblical text.

For Jewish readers and storytellers: There is one story for each week's *sidrah* or Torah portion. The name for each portion is taken from the first significant word or two of that portion. For example, the first *sidrah* is called "Bereishit," which is its first Hebrew word. Bereishit means, "In the beginning..." Each story in this book is based on some aspect of its portion and is designed to be related to it.

For Christian and general readers: The stories are arranged in the order of the first five books of the Bible and are listed by title and the biblical reference on which it is based.

Each story has an introduction that provides background information and gives some indication of what the story is about. Every story is followed by a value lesson, questions for discussion, and story-telling props and tips. Both the "Introducing the Story" and "Values" sections are designed to help the leader prepare rather than for reading to the children. Since I bring my experiences as a rabbi to these stories, in a few cases the value lesson and questions, as well as some elements of the story itself, are told in quite specific Jewish terms. These, of course, can be changed and applied for use by people of all faiths.

Even the simplest props can vastly improve children's involvement in the story. A broom handle can be a magic staff; old hats can be worn by different characters. Typically, I keep all the props in a bag and then, as the story unfolds, I invite a child from the group to hold or wear the particular item mentioned at that point in the story. It is not even necessary for them to act out the story—just holding the props is enough to involve them. The stories can be read as written or told in your own words, with embellishments as you go along.

I hope you enjoy telling these stories as much as I have.

I am grateful to the children of Temple Isaiah for the enthusiastic reception they have given to these stories—for the light in their eyes, and for the smiles on their beautiful faces.

For many years now the Temple Isaiah family has encouraged my writing and given me extra time to bring these stories and other writing to light. I am deeply thankful for their support.

My wife Eileen, our children, Rachel, Deborah, Andrew, and Joseph, have been a constant source of support, help, and love. They, along with our granddaughters, Liana and Michaela, are the center of my story.

This is the fourth book I have done with Behrman House and in each case there has been strong support, a spirit of collaboration, and enormous skill and insight. I am indeed thankful to have had the opportunity to work with such fine people.

1

JUBAL MAKES
SOUNDS FOR GOD

BEREISHIT, Genesis 1:1—6:8

After God created the world, and Adam and Eve left the Garden of Eden, other people were born. One of those people was Jubal. He was the first person to play musical instruments. Neither the Bible nor the Midrash tells us anything else about him. In this story we learn about how Jubal became interested in making music.

Jubal...was the ancestor of all who play the harp and flute. (Genesis 4:21)

Jubal loved to go out of the city and walk in the woods and the fields. He would sit down and listen to the swish of the wind blowing the leaves and the grass. He listened to the "caw-caw" of the crow, the "peep-peep" of the sparrows, and the chirp of the crickets in the tall grass. Sometimes he would go to the beach and listen to the "boom!" of waves crashing against the shore.

He loved these sounds and he thanked God for them. But the city didn't have such beautiful sounds, and when he went home he missed them.

He asked the birds to move back to the city. But they peeped and chattered, asking, "Where would we live? There aren't enough trees for us there. What would we eat?"

Jubal did manage to convince a few crickets, but only a few, and only after he promised them a warm place right next to the kitchen stove. Of course, he couldn't move the big trees or the sounds of the sea back to the city, and that made him feel sad.

One day he came up with a great idea. Maybe he could make some nice sounds. But how? His voice was scratchy and he never could stay in tune, so he decided he wouldn't sing. He did remember seeing some children take a piece of grass, put it between their thumbs, and blow on it, but it only sounded weird. It wasn't the pretty sound he was looking for. He even banged on pots and pans, but that just made noise and not music. Besides, when his mother heard all the racket, she told him to stop.

One day he was playing with some string when one end got caught on a nail. He plucked at it and it made a nice "boing" sound. Next he put several different kinds of string together. That sounded better. Jubal had made a string thing. He began to play it all the time.

Then he tried other ways to make nice sounds. One day he found a hollow piece of wood. He tapped it, he drummed it, and he blew into it. He put holes on top. Now he had a string thing he called a harp and a hollow-wood thing he called a flute. He practiced on them and made up some beautiful songs.

Jubal practiced many hours on his harp and flute. Now he could bring beautiful sounds into the city. Since God had made beautiful sounds for him, he would now be able to make beautiful sounds for God.

That is why the Bible called Jubal the father of all those who play musical instruments. And that is why the Bible also tells us to "Praise God with...strings and flute" (Psalms 150:4).

Values

Each of us has different talents and abilities that we can use to appreciate the wonder and beauty of the world that God has created.

And each of us can use those God-given abilities to make the world a better place. We can be partners with God in creating beauty.

Questions to Discuss

What sounds in nature do you like best?

What is your favorite instrument?

What other ways can you make beautiful sounds for God?

Story-Telling Props and Tips

- a piece of crabgrass to blow against to make sounds
- pots and pans for the children to bang on
- string on a nail in a piece of wood so children can pluck string
- hollow box
- flute or recorder
- autoharp (guitar can be substituted with explanation)

Call on children to try different instruments as they are introduced in the story. Ask children who play the flute or guitar to play a short melody.

2

NIMROD WON'T MIND HIS OWN BUSINESS

NOAH, Genesis 6:9—11:32

Nimrod was Noah's great-grandson. The Torah tells us that he was a mighty man, a hunter. In this story we see how Nimrod hunted for ways to fulfill the laws of justice and kindness which God had given to Noah.

Nimrod...was a mighty hunter before Adonai. (Genesis 10:8-9)

Nimrod was a mighty hunter. You might think that he hunted deer or bears. But Nimrod was a mighty hunter "before God." That made him a special kind of hunter. He hunted for ways to help God. He hunted for things God wanted him to do to help people and to make the world a better place. When Nimrod hunted, he had many adventures.

One day Nimrod was walking in a field. It was a beautiful day. The sun was shining. There were blue, red, and yellow flowers blooming. The birds were singing. A sparrow flew over and sat on his shoulder. Nimrod was having a wonderful walk, whistling as he went, picking an apple from one tree, a pear from another, and blueberries from a bush. He had just started to munch on a juicy pear when the birds began fluttering and darting and making a terrible racket. Then he heard whimpering and crying. When he looked to see what it was, he found a rabbit stuck in a fence. And even worse, there was a hawk circling up in the sky, ready to swoop down on the rabbit. Nimrod went over to the fence, pulled it apart, and the bunny hopped off quickly, soon disappearing down his hole. Nimrod smiled to himself and whistled a lively tune as he walked on.

Another time Nimrod saw two men robbing an old woman. Nimrod ran up to the robbers and yelled at them to leave the woman alone. They asked him, "What do you care about this woman? Mind your own business!" Nimrod told them that robbery and harming people are against God's ways. The robbers warned him that they would beat him up if he didn't leave. Nimrod stood his ground. The two robbers turned and came after him, one with a spear and the other with a knife. Nimrod grabbed a long stick and swung it at them. The robbers realized that Nimrod was ready to protect the woman, so they ran away. The old woman was very frightened, so Nimrod brought her some water and stayed with her until she calmed down.

One day Nimrod was walking in his village and he came across two men fighting over a coat. One yelled, "It's mine!" The other screamed, "No, it's mine!" One man was pulling at it from one side and the other was pulling from the other side until they tore it, making it no good for anyone. Then they started hitting one another and blaming each other for tearing the coat. Nimrod ran over and pulled them apart.

Nimrod was bothered by that argument. He thought that there should be courts of law, where people could go to settle their arguments peacefully. Then people wouldn't fight. So he set up a court. He found wise people who would use the laws of God to decide who is right. He told people from all over that they could come to the court, where things would be decided fairly.

That is why Nimrod was called a mighty hunter before God: he hunted for ways to do God's commandments and he hunted for ways to make the world a better place.

Values

Some of the laws that God taught Nimrod's great-grandfather, Noah, were to be kind to animals and not to rob or murder.

There are many people, and even animals, that need our help. Nimrod hunted or looked for ways to help, and when he saw that he was needed, he didn't wait to be asked. He immediately stepped in to help. We can do the same. We can help animals, we can teach others to be honest, and we can help people settle arguments peacefully.

Questions to Discuss

Did you ever help an animal?

How can you help people to settle disagreements peacefully?

Did you ever stop a fight? Why should you get involved in someone else's fight?

Story-Telling Props and Tips

- flowers, apple, pear, blueberries
- stuffed doll rabbit
- stick
- jacket

3

ABRAM WON'T LIE, SARAI SAVES A BOY

LECH LECHA, Genesis 12:1—17:27

We know that Abram and Sarai were the first to believe that there is only one God. God told them to go to a new land where their family would become a great people serving God. But why did God choose Abram and Sarai? This is a story about what they were like when they were children.

Adonai said, "Go forth from your native land...to the land I will show you." (Genesis 12:1)

God had paid close attention to Abram and Sarai ever since they were children.

Abram and his best friend, Kalman, were always together. They played games, did chores, and studied together. Some people even thought that they were brothers.

One day, Abram, Kalman, and another boy, Baruch, were playing a game of tag. During the game Kalman stepped out of bounds, and when he wouldn't admit that he had, he got into a fight with Baruch. At first the boys pushed one another, but then Baruch slipped, scraped his knee, got angry, and got up swinging at Kalman. Abram ran over to them and told them to stop. Baruch pushed Abram and yelled, "Stop trying to protect your friend."

Abram said, "Kalman doesn't need my protection." He pulled Kalman off to the side and asked, "What are you fighting about? You stepped out of bounds. Let's get on with the game."

Kalman pulled back. "What kind of a friend are you—siding with him?" And he turned away.

Baruch and Kalman kept pushing and hitting one another, so Abram again said, "Come on, stop fighting. Let's get back to the game."

Baruch told Abram to stay out of it: "This is none of your business." And he pushed Abram again. Kalman added, "Abram, get lost."

Abram wouldn't let anyone push him around. He stood his ground. "If both of you are so sure you are right, then why do you want to hit one another when it is so easy to settle it peacefully?"

"Okay, big shot, then who was right?" challenged Kalman, still hoping that Abram would stick up for him.

"Kalman, I told you, you were out of bounds," said Abram. "I saw your foot go over the line."

Kalman was furious and stormed off the field shouting, "You're no friend of mine."

Abram called after him, "If you are such a good friend, would you really want me to lie for you?" Kalman was angry for awhile but finally realized that Abram had done the right thing. They remained good friends.

God had been looking for someone to go to the land of Canaan to teach the world about the One God and to live the way God wants people to live. And God had been paying close attention to Abram. It was very unusual for a boy to be so concerned about fairness that he would say that his best friend was wrong.

God had been keeping an eye on Sarai too. There was a river near Sarai's house, and she would go there to walk along the riverbank, to look at the beautiful flowers on the lily pads, and to listen to the frogs. She also liked to swim. One day Sarai was playing near the river. There had been a storm and the river was very rough and very cold. She was watching the water race along through the rapids when she heard a little boy calling for help. The river was dragging the boy toward the rocks and a waterfall. Quickly she grabbed a branch and jumped into the water. People on the side of the river were yelling at her to come back: "You'll drown trying to save him."

One man ran to get a rope and another went to look for a boat. Meanwhile Sarai swam from rock to rock. One rock was so slippery that she couldn't hold on, and she was swept down the river. Fortunately she was able to hold onto other rocks, and she reached the boy just as he was coming to the rapids and the waterfall. Sarai pushed the branch out in front of the boy, and he grabbed hold of it. Then she pulled him back to the shore.

8

Everybody was amazed that Sarai was strong enough to pull the child out of the river. They were also amazed that she was brave enough even to try to save him. But she answered simply, "I couldn't just let him drown, could I?" Sarai was not only brave, she really cared about people.

God decided that Sarai and Abram were the right people to send to the land of Canaan. Of course Abram and Sarai were still too young to go off on their own. God watched them and saw that Abram continued to seek peace and fairness and Sarai continued to be brave and care for people. When they got older, God made sure they met one another and fell in love. Only after they were married did God send them off on a special mission. God knew that each one of them was very special, but together they had the qualities of justice and courage that would be needed in the future. That was why God said to Abram and his wife Sarai, "Go forth from your native land to the land I will show you."

Values

Each of us has special qualities and abilities. Just as the different qualities of Abram and Sarai were needed by God, so today your many different qualities and abilities are needed to make our world a better place. For example, even children can stop their friends from fighting, or can warn others of danger.

Questions to Discuss

What do you argue about with friends or siblings?

How do you settle disagreements? Do you know how to do it peacefully?

Do you think Abram was right to tell the truth when his friend wanted Abram to side with him?

Story-Telling Props and Tips

- a flower
- toy frog
- a branch or piece of wood

4

Darshanit's Journey to Wisdom

VAYEIRA, Genesis 18:1—22:24

Abraham had long ago left his homeland and settled in the land that God had promised to him. He was well known throughout the land for having faith in the one God of the universe. This story tells how Abraham showed a visitor how to find God.

...pass not away...wash your feet, and recline under the tree...I will fetch a morsel of bread. (Genesis 18:3-5)

Rachman was king over a kingdom that was so beautiful and peaceful that many visitors came to see his land. One of those visitors told Rachman about a man named Abraham who believed in the One God who created the whole world. King Rachman wanted to know where to find this God. He called his daughter, Princess Darshanit, who was not only brave but also very wise and she always tried to learn new things. Rachman told her, "You must go and find Abraham and you must ask him where to find God. For if we can find his God, we will find the way to wisdom, truth, justice, and love."

Darshanit was looking forward to her journey because she loved adventures and she loved to learn. She also loved King Rachman and she did not want to disappoint him.

Darshanit traveled thirty days and thirty nights up and down steep mountains covered with snow, through forests so thick she could hardly see where she was going, and across burning hot deserts.

She was hot, dirty, hungry, and tired when she finally found Abraham encamped on the edge of the wilderness near some trees. Darshanit was surprised that Abraham himself came out to meet her, since he was an important person who had many servants. Immediately she told Abraham that she had come a great distance, across high mountains, through dark forests and burning hot deserts, in order to ask him where to find his God.

Abraham ignored her question and said, "You must be tired from your journey. Please rest here in the shade." Abraham spread out red and yellow blankets and green cushions to make her comfortable. When she felt rested, Darshanit again asked, "Abraham, please tell me where to find your God." Abraham ignored the question again and said, "You must be very dusty and hot. Let me get you some water to wash yourself." So Abraham brought a pan of warm water. Darshanit washed and felt refreshed.

Darshanit again asked Abraham, "My king sent me to ask you an important question. Please, you must tell me, where can he find your God?" This time Abraham simply said, "You must be hungry. I'll bring some food." So Abraham brought bread, cheese, and delicious cake. He said the blessing and they ate.

Darshanit was getting very worried. She wondered, "What will happen if I can't get Abraham to answer me. I don't want to disappoint the king." And again Darshanit pleaded with Abraham to tell her where to find God. And again Abraham ignored her question. The sun was setting. It was getting dark. The air was cool. The big round moon was shining. Stars covered the sky like silver dots spread on black velvet. Abraham told Darshanit to be very quiet. He told her to listen very carefully. It was so still she could hear her own heart beating. An owl hooted in a tree. The light breeze rustled the palm leaves. They looked up and saw the bright stars—thousands of them—looking upon them. Then after a long period of silence she heard Abraham pray in a whisper, "I praise You, my God, who brings on the evening darkness and places the stars in the sky. I thank You my God for this woman who has come to visit me in a search for You." Then Darshanit responded, "Blessed is the God of Abraham, the God found in the kindness of Abraham and in the wonders of the world."

They slowly walked back to the tent. Abraham had told her what she wanted to know. Abraham showed her where God can be found. And she couldn't wait to return home and tell the king.

Values

Abraham was famous for his hospitality, a trait that we have always prized. It is especially important to welcome a new person into a school or neighborhood. Abraham not only was kind to Darshanit; he taught her that God is found in the kind things we do and in our wonder and awe of the natural world.

Questions to Discuss

When you look up at the stars, how do you feel?

Why do you think Abraham took Darshanit to look at the stars?

Why would Abraham need to give Darshanit water for washing?

When people come to your house, how do you think they should be treated?

How do you think we should treat people who have come from far away?

Story-Telling Props and Tips

- blankets
- cushions
- a bowl for water in which to wash
- food and water

5

ELIEZER FINDS
A WIFE FOR ISAAC

HAYEI SARAH, Genesis 23:1-25:18

Abraham and Sarah had a son, Isaac, who would carry on the family tradition of serving God. It was very important that he marry someone who would share in this task of teaching people about the God of justice and kindness. So, Abraham sent his servant and friend Eliezer to find a wife for Isaac. As this story shows, Eliezer's task was not an easy one.

And Abraham said to his senior servant...I will make you swear by the name of Adonai. Go to the land of my birth and get a wife for my son Isaac. (Genesis 24:2, 3, 4)

Early one morning Abraham called his servant Eliezer and said, "I have a very important task for you. Go back to Haran, where I was born, and find a wife for my son Isaac." Abraham gave him ten camels, food for the journey, and much gold and silver.

Eliezer's journey was long and dangerous. He and his helpers, Shoshana, Dorit, and Shlomo, had to cross deserts that were too hot to pass through during the day, so they traveled at night when it was cooler. There were mountains with snow so deep that the travelers were in danger of being buried. But Eliezer wasn't so worried about the dangers of travel. Mostly he wanted to make sure that he would find just the right person for Isaac. Eliezer loved Isaac as if he were his own son, and he loved Abraham as he loved his brother. He was determined to find a suitable mate for Isaac—someone who would make Isaac happy and who Isaac would make happy.

Finally they came to a broad plain where traveling would be easier, but the sun was still very hot there and little water could be found. They traveled for three days and found no water. They traveled two more days and still no water. They hoped they could make it to Ḥaran before their water ran out. Finally they came to a well, and they got off the camels and approached it. A young woman came out to greet them. Eliezer wondered if she would be the right person for Isaac. He asked for water. She said that it was her family's well and since he was a stranger, he couldn't have any water. She put one hand on her hip and with the other she shook her finger at him: "Better move along now. We don't like strangers here."

Eliezer and his helpers got back on their camels and left. Worse than not having the water was the way she treated him. Shoshana said, "Abraham would never send a traveler away." Eliezer added, "There was no way she would be the right wife for Isaac."

Eliezer and his people continued on their journey, but it was so hot they decided to rest under a grove of trees. There was another group resting there as well. A young woman walked by. Eliezer asked her if she had any water they could have. She said, "Sure, but it will cost you one piece of silver for each camel and half a piece of silver for each person." After Eliezer paid her the money and she gave them the water, the young woman walked around them looking at them very closely and laughing the entire time. She couldn't stop laughing. Finally she called other members of her family to look and they also started laughing. Eliezer and his helpers didn't understand what was so funny. Then the young woman asked where they were from. They told her they were from Canaan. She laughed again, saying that their clothes looked funny. She told them that they were entering a very important city and that they should dress in better clothes. She suggested they look at the latest styles in the market just outside the city.

Eliezer and his helpers gave the camels water to drink. Shlomo said sadly, "Whoever heard of selling water to thirsty travelers?" They also looked at one another and wondered what was wrong with their clothes. Dorit shook her head and said, "Selling the water was bad enough, but she was also so rude! Why was the style of our clothes so important to her? She's no wife for Isaac!"

After traveling another three hours, until late in the afternoon, Eliezer and his helpers were again very thirsty. Finally they arrived at another well. Eliezer prayed, "Let this be the place. May there be a young woman who is gracious and helps us with water. May she be the one who will be a good wife for Isaac and Isaac a good husband for her." Just then a young woman came to the well with some sheep. Eliezer stayed off to the side and watched as she carefully gave water to them all. He saw how kind she was, making sure that the lambs got enough to drink. When she was finished, she came over to him. She said she could see that he was very tired and added that she would get water not only for him but also for his camels. After she finished bringing the water, he asked her for her name. "Rebecca," she answered. Eliezer asked if there was a place for them to spend the night. She said she was sure there would be a place for them to stay and also food for his helpers and the animals.

Eliezer knew he had found the wife for Isaac. He told Rebecca and her family why he had come, who Abraham and Isaac were, and what it was like in Canaan. She agreed to go with Eliezer and marry Isaac.

Several weeks later, after the long journey back, they approached Abraham's camp. Rebecca was riding on a camel. The golden sun was setting and the long wisps of clouds in the west looked red and gold. Isaac was walking and meditating in the field during the cool of the evening. When Rebecca saw Isaac walking toward her, she got down off the camel. They embraced and fell in love. Later they had twin sons, Jacob and Esau.

Values

In this story Eliezer and his helpers, Shoshana, Dorit, and Shlomo, were very loyal to Abraham. They were also very brave in traveling such a long way over mountains, deserts, and plains. But they understood that at least as important as being loyal and brave is being kind. Rebecca was especially kind. In this story, being kind means not only helping others, but also being sensitive to their feelings and not making fun of them.

Questions to Discuss

Have you ever been very thirsty? How did you feel when you got a drink of water?

How do you think Eliezer and the people who were with him felt when they were offered water by Rebecca?

How do you think we can be kind to people as Rebecca was?

Did anyone ever make fun of you because of what you wore?
How did you feel?

Do you think it is nice to laugh at people who wear different
clothes or who don't have nice clothes? Why?

Story-Telling Props and Tips

- costume jewelry and "gold" coins for Eliezer to take with him as gifts
- spears and swords to protect themselves
- canteens for water
- articles of old-fashioned clothing

6

ISAAC AND REBECCA DIG WELLS

TOLDOT, Genesis 25:19—28:9

After Isaac and Rebecca were married, there was a famine in Canaan and they traveled to the valley of Gerar to find food. This story tells of the difficulties they faced when they lived among the Philistines in Gerar, and why they finally returned home.

And Isaac dug anew the wells, which had been dug in the days of his father Abraham. (Genesis 26:18)

There was a famine in the land of Canaan and therefore Isaac and Rebecca had to travel to Gerar and live among the Philistines, where there was plenty of food. Unfortunately, some of the Philistines did terrible things. They formed robber bands and would go out to attack caravans—groups of people journeying together through the desert. When they found caravans, they would steal everything, take the women as slaves, and kill the men. When they weren't out robbing people, they spent most of their time sharpening their swords and spears, or showing off to see who had the nicest clothes or the fanciest homes.

Isaac and Rebecca were quiet people who really didn't fit in with the Philistines, but gradually they found themselves wearing fancier and fancier clothes and wanting to move into a bigger house. The Philistines even asked Isaac to join them in their robberies. Isaac was tempted because he and Rebecca would have been able to get even nicer clothes and more gold and silver, but he refused to go with them.

They were especially worried about their sons, Jacob and Esau. Jacob was a quiet boy who kept to himself, but Esau was always getting into trouble. He went out hunting with his bow and arrows and shot lambs and goats belonging to the Philistines. The Philistines insisted that Isaac and Rebecca repay them three animals for every one that Esau killed.

Esau also went out with the Philistines on their robberies and came home with jewelry, clothes, spices, and rare oils that he had stolen. Isaac and Rebecca were very angry and wouldn't let him keep anything that had been stolen. They were very worried that Esau was being influenced more and more by the Philistines. They were also afraid that he might be hurt during one of the attacks. Isaac and Rebecca tried very hard to watch him and keep him close to home, but he always managed to sneak away to join the Philistines in their robberies.

Isaac and Rebecca wanted to leave Gerar and return home as quickly as possible, but there wasn't any food in their homeland. Here in Gerar they had fields where they grew all kinds of fruits and vegetables and they had large flocks of sheep and goats.

But they knew they could not stay among the Philistines any longer. They would simply have to do their best to survive the famine in Canaan. They took as much food as they could, as well as their flocks of sheep and goats, and they left Gerar. They quickly ran out of water, but they remembered that Isaac's father, Abraham, had dug some wells. In trying to remember where the wells were, they talked about Isaac's parents, Abraham and Sarah. They reminded one another about all the things Abraham and Sarah had taught about the One God and about trying to make a just and fair world.

After wandering from place to place, they finally found the spot where the wells had been and they dug a well for water. But as soon as they had dug a well, the Philistines followed them and said that the well belonged to them.

Isaac and Rebecca dug another well. The Philistines came once again and declared that this well also belonged to them. Again Isaac and Rebecca and their family had to leave.

Finally they found out that there was food closer to Isaac's home. They moved there and dug a well. At last the Philistines left them alone. Later on they were able to return home, where God spoke to Isaac saying, "I am the God of your father Abraham. Fear not for I am with you."

Values

Sometimes when we spend a lot of time with people who do the wrong thing, we might be tempted also to do the wrong thing. But just like Isaac and Rebecca, we should return to the wells of our people, to the source of our people's values, and live moral lives.

Questions to Discuss

Were you ever with people who did the wrong thing? Were you tempted to do the wrong thing also? What helped you to do the right thing?

How can your religious beliefs help you in this situation?

Story-Telling Props and Tips

- spears and swords used by the Philistines
- various items such as jewelry and clothes, which Esau might have stolen
- Esau's bow and arrow
- a shovel for digging the well
- a jug or canteen for water

7

BE KIND, HAVE COURAGE, AND THINK FOR YOURSELF

VAYEITZEI, Genesis 28:10—32:3

Jacob and his brother Esau did not get along. After Jacob did several mean things to Esau, and Esau threatened to harm him, Jacob went to stay with his uncle. This story tells about what happened to Jacob on his journey and how Jacob learned to be a better person from his experiences.

Jacob left Beer-sheva and set out for Haran. He came upon a certain place and stopped there for the night...He had a dream. (Genesis 28:10,11,12)

Jacob was going to be away from home by himself for the first time. He was excited but also very frightened. He was now sixteen and his parents, Isaac and Rebecca, were sending him all the way to Haran to stay with his uncle. It was a very long way and would take a long time to get there. His father gave him Carmella, the camel that Jacob loved to ride on. His mother prepared food and clothing for the long trip. They gave him the directions and told him where he should stop for the night.

The first day went well. Jacob was excited about the adventure of it all. The road was clearly marked. There were other travelers to talk to. At night he stayed at an inn, and there he talked with people who had come from many interesting places: spice traders, merchants of cloth

20

and pottery, traders in jewels from Egypt and Lebanon, and even people from Haran. They told him that the road was well marked for the next two days but after that it was difficult to follow and it would be easy to get lost. They said it had already snowed in the mountains and he might not get across if much more snow fell. They also warned him about mountain lions, which would be especially hungry in winter, and about bandits, who watched for travelers to rob and kill. Jacob's spirit of adventure turned to fear.

The next two days went well, as the travelers had told him. But just as they said, the road then turned into a trail with deep ruts. There were few travelers and no inns. It was lucky he still had plenty of food with him.

The first night that he camped out it was cold, but Jacob had plenty of blankets and he felt cozy under them. He dreamed of a ladder going up into the heavens with messengers of God going up and down. The messengers told him that God would protect him and bring him back to his family. They also told Jacob that he would face many challenges on the way to Haran. Finally they told him three wise things: "Be kind. Have courage. Think for yourself."

The next morning it snowed, and by the afternoon there were deep drifts. It was hard for Jacob to see where he was going, so he decided to stop for the night. He couldn't make a fire, but he managed to cover himself and Carmella and he lay down next to her. He ate a dinner of dates and pita bread along with some olives. He worried about feeding Carmella. Because of the snow, there was no place for her to graze. The wind roared and he heard wolves howling not too far in the distance. Once he woke up and thought he saw two big yellow eyes peering at him out of the snowstorm, but he blinked and they disappeared. He shivered in the cold but managed to drift back to sleep.

The morning sun sparkled on the snow, and Jacob led Carmella to places where the snow hadn't covered the ground so Carmella could find grass and straw to eat. Soon they were able to continue on their way.

About midday Jacob came upon an old man calling for help. He went over to the man and found him half frozen. The old man told Jacob that robbers had come during the night and stolen everything he had, including the diamonds and sapphires he kept in a pouch under his shirt. Fortunately, they did not find the large ruby he hid in a secret compartment in his shoe. The old man said he ran off in the storm because the robbers intended to make him their slave. Jacob remembered what he had been told by the messengers in his dream: "Be kind."

He quickly gave the man dry clothes, built a fire, and gave him food to eat. He put the old man on Carmella's back and Jacob walked alongside.

The old man told Jacob that the robbers were sure to try to find him now that the snowstorm was over. Jacob knew that meant he was in danger as well. He certainly couldn't turn the old man over to the robbers. But he was also afraid that he couldn't fight them off. Then he remembered the second piece of wisdom: "Have courage," and he thought about what he could do. He wrapped the old man in blankets and covered him with grass and hay that he found on the side of the road, so that the man looked like a large bundle of Carmella's food. Then he took out his shepherd's slingshot and filled a pouch with round stones.

Just as they feared, the robbers came back. Jacob started whirling his slingshot around and calling out to them that he would not let them have his camel's straw. He warned them that if they got any closer he would shoot the stone at them. They moved closer. He was a very good shot and hit a jug of water they were carrying. The jug broke and the water spilled out. Jacob called out, "One step closer and the next one goes to you." They moved closer. He hit one of the men in the leg, making him howl in pain. The others left, figuring that it wasn't worth the fight just to get some straw.

The old man gave his ruby to Jacob and told him that it had special powers to help him in a time of trouble. Then the man got down from the camel and seemed to disappear over the hill before Jacob could say anything more.

When Jacob reached the gates of the city, they were closed. He banged on the huge gate. After a long time a soldier appeared. Jacob told him he was looking for his uncle Laban. The guard pretended not to know Laban and wouldn't let Jacob in. After begging, and even threatening, Jacob remembered the third piece of wisdom: "Think for yourself." Jacob took out the ruby that the old man had given him. As soon as he held it up in the sun, the ruby sparkled so brightly that it cast a red glow on everything. The guard saw that the gate and walls were red. Jacob looked red and, looking down, the guard saw that his own shoes and clothes were red. The guard was so frightened that Jacob had a ruby with the power to turn everything red that he promised to open the gate if Jacob would only put the ruby away. The gate then opened and the guard bowed deeply as Jacob, riding on Carmella, entered the city, where he finally found his uncle.

Values

Each of us is on a journey in our lives and all of us can learn what Jacob learned: God cares for us and for all people. As we go through life, we, like Jacob, should be alert for the opportunities to help others. No matter what comes our way, we should be kind, have courage, and think for ourselves.

Questions to Discuss

Did you ever take a trip or have an adventure that frightened you? Do you think that God cared for you?

Did you ever have an occasion on which you could be kind to someone? What happened? Did you help? How?

How did Jacob have courage? Did you ever have to do anything that took courage?

Were you ever in a situation when other people were doing the wrong thing and you had to think for yourself and do the right thing? What did you do?

Story-Telling Props and Tips

• rug for sitting on the camel
• food for Jacob
• hats for three traders
• jewelry
• cloth
• paper "ruby" with sparkles

8

No Longer Enemies

VAYISHLAH, Genesis 32:4—36:43

Abraham and Sarah had only one son, Isaac. He married
Rebecca, who gave birth to twin boys. The older of the twins
was Esau. His younger twin brother was Jacob. The two
brothers did not get along. As this story opens, they are about
to meet after having been enemies for many years.

Jacob saw Esau coming...and [they] embraced.
(Genesis 33:1,4)

Jacob sat by the river all night. His twin brother, Esau, who many
years before had threatened to kill him, was only a few miles away and
had an army of 400 men. Jacob, who had flocks and herds and a large
family, was very frightened. If Esau killed him, what would become of
his family? He kept thinking of a way to escape, but how could he? He
couldn't run away. His family and all the animals traveled too slowly. He
wondered if he and his shepherds could fight Esau. But how could they
do that? There were only a few of them and they had no real weapons.
They were shepherds, not soldiers.

Jacob thought about how he had first gotten into this mess. He
recalled his childhood. Esau was a gifted runner. He could run long dis-
tances without getting tired and he could run very fast. He was also very
strong. Jacob remembered that when Esau was out with the flocks, Esau
could not only carry a tired lamb across his shoulders, he could also
swing a lost sheep on his back and carry it as if it were a big sack. Jacob
remembered how everybody liked Esau. He could make them laugh

with his funny stories. He remembered how their father seemed to like Esau better than him and how Esau would hunt and bring his father deer and birds.

Jacob was very different. He wasn't especially strong and he couldn't run very fast. He never told jokes—either he couldn't remember one or he would tell it all wrong and no one would laugh. He was quiet but he was helpful, especially to his mother. Jacob remembered how he had learned to cook, which was unusual for a boy to do in those days. He liked to read and study. He remembered how his mother seemed to like him better than she liked Esau. And, of course, Jacob enjoyed his mother's attention. He'd go to extra trouble to help her; running errands for her and spending time talking to her when she was lonely.

He thought back to all the arguments he had had with Esau and how he hated it when people laughed at Esau's jokes. He hated it when Esau was cruel to the goats, throwing rocks at them just to see them run in all directions. He also remembered how Esau and he were mean to one another—how Esau stole Jacob's special collection of unusual rocks and how Jacob told their mother every time Esau did anything wrong.

Jacob also remembered stealing his father's special blessing. In those days it was customary for the father to give a special blessing and an extra share of money to the oldest son. Esau was the oldest and should have received the blessing and the money, but Jacob, by pretending to be Esau, tricked his blind father into giving the blessing and the money to him. Esau was so angry he had threatened to kill Jacob. That was the final straw. Jacob ran away to his Uncle Laban's house and the brothers hadn't seen each other since.

In the years that followed, Jacob married, had many children, and accumulated large flocks of sheep and goats. Now they would meet tomorrow and Jacob was terrified that Esau would kill him. He no longer hated Esau. He was no longer sure that he even disliked him. He wasn't even angry with him any more. Jacob was just afraid of him.

The only thing Jacob could think of doing was to send Esau gifts to show that he had no hard feelings and that he was sorry for having done all those mean things. So Jacob sent valuable sheep and goats, as well as gold and silver, to Esau.

Esau, who was in his own tent, had also stayed up all night thinking about their meeting. He wasn't afraid that Jacob would harm him, but he felt very bad about having threatened to kill Jacob. He hadn't really meant it, but he had been very angry at the time. Esau had frightened his parents into sending Jacob far away to his uncle's house. At the time he had been glad to be rid of his brother. Esau was no longer angry with Jacob for tricking him. He didn't need his father's blessing. He had become rich on his own, so the blessing didn't matter now. Esau even prepared some gifts for Jacob—special flocks and gold jewelry.

Soon it was morning. Esau sat in his tent waiting nervously. Jacob set out to meet Esau. As he approached Esau's tent, he kept stopping and bowing to show his respect. Jacob had no idea what to expect. He was terrified that Esau or his men would grab him and kill him on the spot. Finally, when he got closer, he saw Esau coming toward him. Jacob was so frightened that he wasn't sure whether Esau was coming to greet him or to attack him. When Esau was right in front of him, he saw that Esau's arms were extended to hug Jacob. Jacob hugged him back.

They sat in Esau's tent and talked for a while and then parted. The brothers never did become friends, but at least now they weren't enemies. They didn't see one another again until their father, Isaac, died. Then together they buried him.

Values

Those who have brothers and sisters sometimes get into arguments with them. They might sometimes be angry with them. They might even think that their parents love their brother or sister more than them. But they should realize that parents love all their children. Brothers and sisters should try to understand that, like Jacob and Esau, they can overcome the anger of the moment and learn to understand one another and get along better with one another.

Questions to Discuss

Do you ever think your parents sometimes like your brother or sister better than you?

Do you sometimes fight with your brother or sister? Do you ever do mean things to one another? How do you make up?

Story-Telling Props and Tips

• sneakers
• a hunting hat and a spear or bow and arrow for Esau
• books and cooking utensils for Jacob
• gifts the brothers gave to one another

9

KINDNESS, WISDOM, AND DREAMS

VAYEISHEV, Genesis 37:1—40:23

Jacob gave his son, Joseph, a special coat of many colors because Joseph was his favorite son. Joseph also had dreams that he would be the most important person in his family. These dreams made his brothers angry. One day Joseph was sent to check on his brothers who were tending sheep. He lost his way until two mysterious people helped Joseph to find his brothers.

And a certain man found him, and behold, he was wandering in the field. (Genesis 37:15)

When Joseph was young, his brothers would ignore him. If he wanted to go with them out to the fields or join in playing their games, they would say he was too little. Still, he hung around them and listened to them talking about their wonderful adventures. He listened to them tell about how they found a place where water came up out of the rocks. He heard the tale of how they saw rainbows in the mountains and how they fought off mountain lions to prevent them from attacking the sheep. But no matter how much he begged, they would still not let him come with them to the fields.

Joseph's brothers would also bully him. When he took out his toys and games, his brothers would take them away from him, saying, "You are a baby playing with baby things." After a while he learned that he could play with only one thing at a time and he had to leave everything else safely hidden for another time. He was sure that some day they would feel sorry for being mean to him.

One day Jacob told him to go find his brothers. "Tell me how they are doing," he said. Joseph was overjoyed and he set out right away. He brought water and put food in his knapsack. Then he put on his special coat of many colors. His father had given it to him because Joseph was his favorite. Joseph set out on his adventure, feeling sure that his brothers were doing exciting things that he could be a part of for at least a little while.

He walked all morning and couldn't find them. Soon he felt hot and tired and he sat down to rest. The more he walked, the less sure he was of where he was. He didn't know how to find his brothers. Finally he had to admit to himself that he was lost. He had only a little food and water left, and he was very frightened. He was afraid that he wouldn't find his brothers. Even worse, he was afraid that he wouldn't be able to find his way home. Most of all, he was afraid his brothers would make fun of him if they found out that he had gotten lost. They would say he was just a little kid who couldn't do anything right.

Just as he was about to give up and try to find his way home, he saw an old woman slowly making her way over a hill. Joseph ran up to her and asked her if she had seen his brothers and their sheep. She told him that she hadn't seen his brothers. Joseph noticed that the old woman looked very thin and pale. He offered her some food and water. She ate, drank, and then got up to leave, saying, "For your kindness, I will send someone who will show you the way." She added, "God will always watch over you and will give you the special ability to interpret dreams." Joseph thanked her but wondered how she could possibly make such promises.

No sooner had she left than Joseph was startled to see a man, wearing a tattered coat and no shirt, appear out of nowhere. He was even more surprised when the man said, "I know that you are able to interpret dreams." Before Joseph could answer, the man told him his dream.

"I dreamed that there was a long table in the middle of the forest and it was all set for a great party. There were big pots and baskets full of food and large jugs filled with sweet wine. As soon as all the food was placed on the table, a flock of birds swooped down and took all the food. I had this dream only one time. But later I had another similar dream. This time there were the same pots and baskets of food and jugs of wine, but the people put only a little at a time on their plates. Then they happily ate and enjoyed the feast. What does this mean?"

Joseph answered, "There is great wisdom in your dreams. In the first dream the people put out all their food even though they saw the birds. But in the second dream they kept most of the food in the baskets, away from the birds, and took out only what they were going to eat at that time. This shows that sometimes we have to save for the future." The old man praised Joseph for his wisdom. Joseph just smiled, remembering how he played with only one toy at a time so his brothers wouldn't take them. Joseph wondered if God had been guiding him and teaching him.

"If you want to find your brothers, take the path through those trees over there. Then go down into the valley and you will find them there." Joseph thanked the man and said to him, "I would give you my coat, but this is a special coat my father gave me and I can't give it away. But here is my shirt; I have another at home." Joseph took off his shirt and gave it to the man. Joseph was now so happy to be on his way that he sang to himself, thinking that he would soon be able to share in his brothers' adventures. He found the path and walked under the trees in the shade, which became darker and darker until he found himself deep in a forest.

As soon as he sat down on a large moss-covered rock, he was astonished to see the old woman standing before him. "You have again been very kind," she said, "and, as you can see, you do know how to interpret dreams. Always remember to be kind. As long as you are kind, God will enable you to interpret dreams wisely." Then she added, "See how dark this forest is?" Joseph looked around and nodded. The old lady continued, "You will go through a dark time in your life, but just as you found your way when you were lost today, you will find your way again. Always remember that God is with you." With those words she disappeared. Then, as soon as Joseph stood up from the rock, the dark forest also disappeared and he entered a beautiful green and sunny valley, where he found his brothers.

Values

Even though Joseph was tired and frightened, he helped the old woman and the man without being asked. There are times when we can offer to help people even before they ask. And when we are kind to others, kindness and help can come to us in unexpected ways.

Questions to Discuss

Why do you think Joseph's brothers were mean to him? How did Joseph react to their meanness?

Why do you think Joseph was kind to the old man?

Are there ever times when you can help someone who needs help even though the person has not asked? Why might we want to help someone who needs help before they ask? How could you help someone?

Story-Telling Props and Tips

• toys
• coat of many colors
• baskets and pots for food
• brightly colored shirt
• knapsack with food

10

JOSEPH KEEPS HIS DREAMS ALIVE

MIKETZ, Genesis 41:1—44:17

Joseph, who had earlier dreamed that he would be the most important person in his family, now explains Pharaoh's dreams. As a reward for this, Pharaoh appoints Joseph as overseer of the land of Egypt. This makes Joseph the most important person in Egypt, except for Pharaoh. When Joseph's brothers come to Egypt to buy grain during a great famine in Canaan, he recognizes them but they do not recognize him. This story tells of some of Joseph's troubles before he arrived in Egypt. It also explains what happened to Joseph that made the dreams of his youth come true.

Pharaoh said to Joseph, "See, I put you in charge of all the land of Egypt." (Genesis 41:41)

When Joseph was a boy, he had many dreams. He dreamed that he would do incredible things in his life and that he would be very important to his family. One day his father told him to go out and find his brothers, who were taking care of the sheep. His father wanted to know how his sons were. Joseph put on the special coat of many colors that his father had given him, because he was his father's favorite son. Then he went out to look for his brothers. Now Joseph's brothers did not like him, because he was their father's favorite and because he was always telling on them when they did something wrong. When Joseph reached them, they decided to get rid of him, so they sold him as a slave to a passing Ishmaelite caravan.

Poor Joseph was devastated. It was bad enough being away from home with strange people; it was bad enough that he was being taken far away from his family; but the fact that his brothers had done this terrible thing to him was the worst of all. Maybe he annoyed them sometimes and did things they didn't like. Maybe he borrowed things of theirs without asking. Maybe he even told their father some of the things they had done wrong. He could understand if they were angry with him, but to do this? And what about his father; he must be very worried about him. What would the brothers even tell him? He was so sad that he cried all night.

The Ishmaelites treated Joseph well. They gave him enough to eat and a comfortable place to sleep. After a few days Joseph felt a little better. He kept thinking: "The dreams God has given to me will come true. Some day I will do incredible things in my life and be important to my family. Some day those dreams will come true." He repeated this again and again.

Other times he would think of ways to escape. When they came to a mountainous area, Joseph decided to run away. He took a little food and water and, when it was dark, he sneaked away from the camp. He thought he could travel at night and follow the stars the way his father had taught him. As soon as he was away from the camp, he tried to get his bearings, but he couldn't figure out which stars were which and how he should go. When his father explained the system, he made it sound so simple, but it wasn't simple at all. Joseph panicked. He was lost. Fortunately, when the sun rose in the morning he could determine which way was east. But as the sun rose higher and higher in the sky, the day grew hotter and hotter. Joseph got thirsty and soon drank the last of his water. He also finished the little bit of food he had. All the while he continued to wander toward his home. He kept repeating to himself that the dreams God had given him would be fulfilled, that he would do incredible things in his life, and that he would be very important to his family. Just when he was afraid that he would die of thirst, he came upon a woman herding sheep. She gave him water and food, and she pointed out the direction to his home. But soon that bit of food and water were gone. Later that day he was found by the Ishmaelites, who had been looking for him. They were very angry with him for running away. When they brought him back to their caravan, they tied him up so he couldn't get away again. Joseph had a hard time keeping his hope up. He kept telling himself that everything would be all right, but it was hard to believe that it was true.

About a week after the Ishmaelites picked him up, a Midianite caravan passed and the two groups stopped to talk. When Joseph heard that the Midianites were going back to his homeland, he begged the women who brought him his food to untie the ropes that held him. Then he hid in the caravan of Midianites. But no sooner had the Midianites set out than they changed direction and headed to Egypt. Now they would sell him into slavery in Egypt.

Joseph tried not to be discouraged, but nothing seemed to work out for him. It seemed that he was destined to end up in Egypt, and if he was to be an Egyptian slave, it was hard to understand how the dreams God had given him could come true. Still, he tried to hope.

As soon as the Midianites arrived in Egypt, they sold him to a man named Potiphar. Joseph was very frightened. He had no idea what Potifar would make him do and how he would treat him. But every night, no matter how bad his situation seemed, Joseph always told himself that some day and somehow, all the dreams God gave him would come true.

Now God gave Joseph not only important dreams, but also the ability to understand other people's dreams. Soon even Pharaoh, the king of Egypt, heard that Joseph could understand dreams and he asked Joseph to explain his dreams. Joseph explained them so wisely that Pharaoh appointed Joseph to be the overseer of the land of Egypt. He helped to prepare the Egyptians for the coming famine. When Joseph's own family came down to Egypt to buy food, he took care of them. And so it was only after Joseph had courage and believed in himself, and only after Joseph explained the dreams of others, that the dreams God had given him could come true. Joseph did do very important things in his life and he became very important to his family.

Values

Like Joseph, each of us has dreams—dreams of doing important things for ourselves and the world, and dreams of being important to our family. Like Joseph, it sometimes seems as if those dreams cannot possibly come true. But if we are able to keep our dreams alive, as Joseph did, then like Joseph, we can have hope that they will come true.

In addition, Joseph went through very serious hardships and was still able to improve the lives of others. We, in our lives, may have to go through difficulties, but we may find that we are still able to help others.

Questions to Discuss

What kinds of dreams have you had? Did you ever try to understand what those dreams meant?

Did you ever try to understand or interpret the dreams of other people?

Story-Telling Props and Tips

• hats to wear, indicating the different characters: Joseph, his brothers, an Ishmaelite, a Midianite, Potiphar, and Pharaoh.
• a small bottle of water and some food for Joseph

11

DINAH, HER BROTHERS, AND THE BABA GANUSH ROBBERS

VAYIGASH, Genesis 44:18—47:27

After Joseph's family came to Egypt, they were allowed to live in an area called Goshen. We are told that they were put in charge of Pharaoh's flocks. This story fills in the gaps about what the brothers and their sister, Dinah, did in Goshen.

Pharaoh said to Joseph, "...if you know any capable people, put them in charge of my livestock." (Genesis 47:5,6)

After Joseph became an important leader in Egypt, his brothers came down to live near him. Pharaoh agreed to let them live in Goshen and he put the brothers to work taking care of his cattle. Pharaoh said to Joseph, "Assign your bravest people to watch over my cattle. Make sure none of the cattle are lost or stolen or I will send your family away." There were many, many dangers. Joseph knew it would be a hard job, but he wanted his family to be near him.

Early one morning when Joseph's family was just waking up, they heard the cattle bellowing and the sheep bleating, "ba-a-a, ba-a-a." They were making a terrible racket and soon were running in all directions. His brother Judah went to see what was happening. Off to the side he saw a pack of wolves creeping up on the flocks. Judah was frightened. He knew that wolves are very good hunters and he was afraid they would attack the sheep. Sure enough, when Judah got closer, he could see that the wolf pack was closing in on one black and white sheep. Judah quickly skirted the edge of the camp, moving closer to the wolves and approaching them from the side. Judah, who had won slingshot contests, took out his long thong slingshot, put a smooth stone in it, and whipped it around in the air faster and faster. He then shot it at the lead wolf. He missed. Judah couldn't believe it. He never missed! The stone hit the ground just in front of the wolf, which was so startled that it ran away. The other wolves then followed him. Judah breathed a big sigh of relief.

A few weeks later the brothers saw a large band of robbers creeping over the hill in the moonlight. Benjamin recognized them as members of the feared Baba Ganush band. He told the other brothers to get their spears and slingshots ready, and then he told them his plan. The brothers and their sister, Dinah, crept among the cattle, hiding behind them. They watched as the robbers, who had ropes, nets, and spears, moved closer and closer to the flocks. As soon as the robbers were about to grab the first lamb, the brothers jumped out from behind the goats and cows, made bloodcurdling shrieks, and banged pots and pans. Dinah had a big drum that she beat so loudly it sounded like thunder. The Baba Ganush band were terrified. They thought there must be some dark magic at work since they could hear thunder but there were no clouds in the sky. The brothers shot stone after stone at the robbers, who ran away imagining that there must be a hundred people protecting the flocks.

Later that week a man came to visit the brothers. He wore a tall hat, a long robe, and very big shoes. The man said that he wanted to buy the newborn calves. The brothers said that the cattle all belonged to Pharaoh and they couldn't sell any of them. The man said that Pharaoh wouldn't know. Since Pharaoh counted only the cattle he had originally entrusted to their care, he wouldn't know anything about new calves that had been born. Two of the brothers, Simeon and Levi, said they should sell the calves. "Look at us," they argued. "We are poor. We came from Canaan and are penniless. If we sold some of Pharaoh's cattle, we could have a new start in life. Besides, no one would know." But Reuven said that they would all know and that God would know that they had been dishonest. Finally all the brothers agreed and sent the man away.

Everything was peaceful for a long time. Summer passed and so did the fall. Finally winter set in. Then something very unusual happened. It snowed. The brothers, who had seen snow only a few times, were delighted but also worried. The animals were restless. They did not know what this cold, white, slippery stuff was that was falling from the sky. The snow got deeper and the temperature got colder. One of the brothers said they should leave the cattle and try to find better shelter for themselves. After all, there was very little wood to be found, and they could not make a big enough fire to keep warm. The wind was howling and the brothers were afraid of freezing to death. Issachar told them that first they had to watch the flocks. That was their job and that is what they would do. He told them to lead all the cattle into a deep valley where there was no wind. Then he told them to bring in as many sheep as would fit into their tent. Then they would all squeeze into the tent with the sheep. Between the warmth of the sheep and the thick wool of the sheep's coats, everyone would be warm. When the storm was over they quickly checked on the cattle in the valley and found them all happily chewing on grass that poked through the snow.

The brothers lived happily in Goshen, taking care of Pharaoh's cattle for a very long time.

Values

Each of these people had different abilities and had courage in a different way. Each of them overcame some fear or temptation. Sometimes we too are afraid. Sometimes we are also tempted to do the wrong thing and it takes courage and imagination to find the way we should go.

Questions to Discuss

Were you ever asked to take care of something? How did you feel?

Did anyone ever urge you to lie or to take something that didn't belong to you? What did you do?

Have you heard the expression "to tell a white lie"? What does it mean? Is it okay to tell these kinds of lies?

Story-Telling Props and Tips

- a slingshot
- a spear
- pots and pans
- whistles, noisemaker, drum
- gold or silver coins

- handful of white confetti for snow
- robe and shoes for the visitor

This story lends itself to very dramatic telling. The teller and the children can make the appropriate sounds for the cattle, pots and pans, and the howling wind.

12

THE HEALING PEAR

VAYEHI, Genesis 47:28—50:26

Before Jacob died, he gave a blessing to each of his sons. When he blessed his son Naphtali, he said that Naphtali ". . . gives goodly words." Since the Torah doesn't explain what this means, this story about another man who was named Naphtali teaches us what "goodly words" might mean.

Naphtali...gives goodly words. (Genesis 49:21)

Long ago and in a land far away there lived a king who had three daughters. His two oldest daughters married rich princes. Their marriages made the king very happy. But the youngest daughter, Hanna, insisted on marrying a poor man named Naphtali, whom she loved dearly. The king was very angry that she would marry someone who was not a prince and who was poor, so he sent them to live at the far end of the kingdom. They were very happy together but Hanna missed her father.

As the king grew older, he developed a mysterious disease and he became blind. He called upon all the doctors, all the magicians, and all the sorcerers in the kingdom to try to cure his blindness. None of them was successful. The king was desperate. Then one day a traveler told the king that there was a wise woman who knew of a magic pear tree whose fruit could cure blindness. The traveler added that only those who were very brave and very good could find it. The king immediately sent out a proclamation to all the princes of the kingdom: "The person who brings back the healing pear will inherit half my kingdom and a great chest of jewels filled with diamonds, rubies, and emeralds."

Immediately the two princes who had married the king's daughters went off to find the wise woman. They traveled for thirty days and thirty nights across mountains deep with snow, forests filled with bears, jungles teeming with tigers, and deserts overflowing with scorpions. They even had to fight off dragons and lions.

Finally they came to the wise woman. She was sitting under a tree at the edge of a village. She told them they must walk through the village, where they would be faced with three tests. If they passed the three tests, they would find the tree with the healing pear on the other side of the village. If they did not pass the tests, the ground on the other side of the village would open up and they would disappear forever. She told them that only those who are very brave and very good would pass the tests. "Do you have the courage to try?" she asked. They asked what the tests were. The wise woman only told them that the tests were unlike any they had ever undergone. They said that since they had met so many tests already in their lives, they were sure they could meet the challenge of these tests too.

The two princes entered the town, which looked much like any other town. There was a marketplace and people shopping. There was a beggar, as in other towns. They passed two people arguing and a little boy who was sick and crying for his mother. Nothing unusual about this town, they thought. They kept waiting for the test. Perhaps someone would jump out from behind a building and attack them. As they neared the end of the town with nothing happening, they were puzzled and relieved. They figured that they would soon come to the tree with the healing pears. But just as they reached the end of the town, the ground opened up and they disappeared.

Other people tried to pass the tests as well, but they too failed. Some did not even reach the wise woman.

Naphtali did not hear the king's proclamation until long after it was made, because he lived so far away from the palace. He immediately decided that he would to try to find the healing pear. Hanna wanted to be reunited with her father, and Naphtali thought that if he could cure the king, the king might welcome them back.

Naphtali traveled for thirty days and thirty nights across mountains deep with snow, forests filled with bears, jungles teeming with tigers, and deserts overflowing with scorpions. He fought off dragons and lions. Finally he came to the wise woman, who told him he must walk through the village, where he would meet three tests. She told Naphtali that only those who are both very brave and very good would be successful. The wise woman told him that if he passed the tests, he would find the healing pear. If he failed, he would disappear. Like the princes, Naphtali asked what the tests were, and the wise woman gave him the same answer: the test was unlike any he had ever undergone. Naphtali decided to try.

He entered the town. When he saw the beggar, he gave him a few coins and spoke a few kind words, "goodly words," telling the beggar not to give up hope for a better life. When he saw the men fighting, he went over to them and helped them to settle their argument peacefully so that they walked away as friends. He had spoken kind words, "goodly words," to them. When he saw the sick little boy crying for his mother, he dried the boy's tears and comforted him as he took his hand and walked him home. Again he spoke kind words, "goodly words." When Naphtali arrived at the end of the town, he saw a path with beautiful flowers. He took the path, which went through a meadow, until he came to a clearing. In the middle of the clearing was a pear tree with a beautiful pear. The wise woman was sitting under the tree. She told Naphtali, "Because you were both brave in crossing mountains and deserts, and you were good in that you were kind to people, you are worthy of the healing pear. Use it wisely."

In an instant Naphtali was at the palace. At first the king would not even see him. Then Naphtali sent word that he had the healing pear. The king was so anxious to be cured and so amazed that Naphtali would risk his life to try to cure him, that the king welcomed him warmly. Of course the healing pear that Naphtali brought did cure the king's blindness and he could see once again. Naphtali and Hanna moved to the palace. Many years later, after the king died, Naphtali ruled the kingdom bravely and with kindness.

Values

The qualities of kindness and courage mark true nobility. Providing for the poor, helping to resolve conflict, and comforting the suffering are the true test of character.

Questions to Discuss

Why did Naphtali want to reach the pear tree? What did that show about him?

Why did Naphtali succeed in reaching the healing pear when the princes failed?

Did you ever have the opportunity to help the poor, help make peace between people, or comfort someone? What did you do?

Story-Telling Props and Tips

This story should be told in the "Once upon a time" fairy tale style, in a very dramatic manner.

- pear
- wise woman's hat
- crowns for princes
- larger crown for the king
- flowers

13

ZIPPORAH'S BROTHER

SHEMOT, Exodus 1:1—6:1

After Moses struck an Egyptian taskmaster for beating an Israelite, he had to flee Egypt. He went out into the desert, where he met a man named Reuel. (He is also called Jethro later in the Book of Exodus.) He married Reuel's daughter, Zipporah. While living with Zipporah's family, Moses learned something very important about names, especially the names used for God.

Moses said to God, "When I come to the Israelites and say to them, 'The God of your fathers has sent me to you,' and they ask me, 'What is His name?' what shall I say to them?" And God said to Moses: "Eh'yeh-Asher-Eh'yeh (I AM THAT I AM)...This shall be My name forever. (Exodus 3:13-15)

Moses' wife was named Zipporah. She had six sisters and a brother. With so many children, it wasn't easy for her parents to keep track of all eight of them. They gave each daughter a name, and each daughter used that name all the time. None of this is surprising—after all, most people keep the same name all the time, don't you?

But Zipporah's brother was different. Since he was the only son, he could use any name he wanted to and everyone would still know whom they were talking about. So his parents let him choose his names. Not only that, but he was allowed to change his name at any time. He really had fun trying out new names. On a day when Zipporah's brother wanted to be considered strong, he took the name "Gibor," meaning strong. Sure enough, he looked at his muscles and they seemed bigger. On a day when he wanted to be considered very important, he called himself "Kochav," meaning, "star." Sure enough, he felt taller and people paid him compliments. On a day when he wanted to let people know how smart he felt, he gave himself the name "Hacham," which means "wise." And in this case, too, he thought he said all kinds of wise and important things. It seemed to him that when he used a name, he could become what the name meant.

Sometimes he used everyday names too, and on those days he felt quite average.

Moses thought this system of names was wonderful. In fact, he and Zipporah's brother had a lot of fun together choosing names. They even made up unusual names like Zefonan, Yupidoodle, and Orbitsupdownallaround. Then they felt silly and they laughed and laughed.

Moses learned something very important while he was having fun helping Zipporah's brother choose names. He learned that when God began to speak to Moses, God used different names: El Shaddai, Adonai, Elohim, and even "Eh'yeh-Asher-Eh'yeh—I Am That I Am." But Moses understood that even though there were many different names for God, there was only One God. Whatever name God used, Moses would understand that it was the One God who was speaking to him.

Values

In the Bible and in our prayers there are many different names for God: *YHVH* (pronounced *Adonai* by Jews), *Elohim*, *El*, *Shaddai*, and *Yah* are just a few. All these and other names for God are just different ways of speaking about God and to God. No matter what name is used, God is still the One God who created and rules the universe and who cares about us.

Questions for Discussion

What names would you like to have in addition to the name your parents gave you? Why?

Story-Telling Props and Tips

Obtain or make a different hat for each of the names Zipporah's brother used. As the name is mentioned, ask a child to come forward to wear that hat.

For older children you may want to point out the different names for God even as they appear in English. See Genesis 1:1 for *God*; 2:4 for *Lord God*; and 17:1 for *God Almighty*.

14

MOSES GOES EXPLORING

VA'EIRA, Exodus 6:2—9:35

At the time that Moses was born, Pharaoh had ordered all Israelite boys to be drowned in the Nile River. Instead, Moses' mother placed him in a basket and floated it down the river in the hope that someone would find it and care for the infant. It so happened that an Egyptian princess found him and raised him in Pharaoh's palace. Later, Moses was called by God to free the Israelites from slavery. Moses became discouraged when the Israelites themselves wouldn't listen to him. God assured Moses that the people would be freed. Why did God choose Moses out of all the people? This story tells about Moses' qualities when he was a boy, which showed God that Moses would be the one who could lead the people.

God spoke to Moses, saying, "Go and tell Pharaoh King of Egypt to let the Israelites depart from his land."
(Exodus 6:10-11)

When Moses was growing up in Pharaoh's palace, he had a wonderful time. The palace had long halls, and there were lots of secret hiding places. There were dogs and cats to play with and there were even

46

monkeys, which he taught to do tricks. And, best of all, he had his very own horse.

Any time he wanted to go someplace, like down to the great River, he could get on his horse and go. He often played with Egyptian children. They knew that he came from the Israelites, but they didn't seem to care. The princess who raised him was very nice, and Pharaoh never bothered him.

As he got older, he went to see more and more places on his own. One day he took some food, got on his horse, and went off exploring. All his life he could see great buildings being constructed off in the distance, but he had never seen them up close.

Soon Moses arrived at the site. He was amazed at how big the buildings were. He also noticed that there were hundreds, maybe even thousands, of people carrying heavy rocks, moving soil, and cutting tremendous stones. Then he looked more closely at the people. They looked very thin. Some of them begged for food. Some looked sick. Sometimes they just passed out in the hot sun because there was no water there. The guards would whip them until they either stood up or died.

Moses started to shake in anger. He had always been told that the slaves were well treated and that they lived a good life. They had treated *him* well but had lied to him about how they treated his people. Now he realized that he didn't understand at all what slavery meant. The Israelites he had seen in the palace were just ordinary workers. He now knew that he didn't understand how badly the rest of his people were being treated. He was enraged and confused. He wanted to help but he didn't know what to do.

Moses turned his horse around and rode sadly back to the palace. At first he tried to forget what he had seen. He tried to pretend it was a bad dream. He told himself that there was nothing he could do. But still he was troubled. He couldn't sleep at night because he kept thinking of ways that he might help.

Moses' best friend was one of the Israelite workers in the palace. He was an older boy, named Elya. When Moses told him what he had seen, Elya sadly replied that there was nothing Moses could do. There were too many who were hungry; there were too many who were thirsty. Pharaoh would not allow the slaves to be given any help, and Moses would only get into trouble for even mentioning it.

But Moses could not stop thinking about it. He had some friends among the Egyptian children. Ra was one of his best buddies. When Moses told him what he had seen Ra said, "Mind your own business. You can't do anything. Just be glad you have it good and enjoy life." Moses was furious. How could Ra tell him to enjoy life when his people were being treated so badly?

Moses was so upset that he could not eat or sleep. He lost weight. His face looked gray. An old Israelite woman, whose name we do not know, worked in the palace. She took him aside and asked him what was troubling him. He found a place where no one would hear them and he told her everything he had seen. As Moses told his story, he could see in her deep black eyes that she was a woman of great wisdom and courage. She said, "Moses, you are free. And you must help our people." Moses heard the determination in her voice. She went on: "Pharaoh isn't going to free the slaves and stop the building in his honor. But you must try to help. You must try to do what you can. This is my plan." Then she told him exactly what he must do.

The next day Moses spoke to the man in charge of construction. The man complained to him that the building was behind schedule because he couldn't get the slaves to work faster. Moses said, "Maybe if you gave them enough food and water they would be better workers." The foreman kept saying that the people were slaves and he shouldn't treat them any better. Moses kept telling him that the slaves would work better if they had enough to eat and drink. It wasn't easy to convince him, but the man in charge finally figured that since Moses was a prince in Pharaoh's house, he should listen to him.

That is how Moses helped his people long before he could free them. It was because of Moses' sensitivity to the suffering of his people that God asked Moses to lead the Israelites out of slavery to freedom.

Values

Even though he could not free the Israelites at first, Moses was at least able to help them. He learned from the Israelite woman what our sages taught many years later: We are not required to heal every hurt and end every injustice, but we are required to try. For whoever saves one life, it is as if he or she has saved the whole world.

Questions for Discussion

How do you think Moses felt when he saw the slaves?

Why was helping so important to Moses?

How do you help others?

Story-Telling Props and Tips

- a stuffed doll dog or cat
- monkey
- a hobbyhorse or a box covered with a cloth or small rug, to serve as a horse

When you reach the part of the story where the old woman says she has a plan, ask the children, before continuing with the story, what they think it might have been?

15

EARRINGS FROM THE EXODUS

BO, Exodus 10:1—13:16

When the Israelites left Egypt, they accepted gold and silver from the Egyptians. This story tells how one family acquired a special pair of gold earrings and what happened to those earrings over the centuries.

The Israelites...acquired from the Egyptians jewels of silver and gold. (Exodus 12:35)

An old woman sat in a chair in her living room, much like the one in your own home. She held up a single gold earring and said, "This is one of a pair of earrings which has been in my family for thousands of years. It comes from the time of the Exodus. I want to tell you how we got the pair of earrings and why we have only one left." Then she told this story:

"Long ago, at the time of the Exodus from Egypt, when my great, great, great, great, great, great grandmother, Shira, was a little girl, she and her family were slaves in Egypt. She had big brown eyes, skin darkened from the sun, and one torn dress which she wore all the time. Shira and her family lived in a little shack near a big house. Her mother was a slave for the lady in the house. Her father moved large stones for a building that was being built in the Pharaoh's honor. Life was very hard, but Shira had a loving family, so she was a happy child. They called her 'Shira,' which means 'song' in Hebrew, because she was always singing.

"In the spring of the year when she turned eight, there was a lot of excitement. There was a man named Moses, who said God would free the Israelites from slavery and bring them to their own land. Strange things happened: the river ran red like blood; there were frogs all over the Egyptian houses and farms; there were terrible hailstorms. Moses said these things were caused by God to force the Egyptians to free them. When Shira was supposed to be sleeping, she listened to the grownups talking far into the night. Her parents always believed in God and now they also believed what Moses was saying. But other people thought life would be worse if they left. They were afraid that Moses would drag them out to the desert and they would all die of thirst.

"Soon the time came for them to leave Egypt. The great day they had hoped and prayed for had arrived. Everyone was excited—but also worried. Would they actually leave? Would the Egyptians stop them? Would the Egyptians make them suffer even more because they tried to get away? Everyone had a different fear and everyone was talking at once. Then there was a knock on the door. Everyone grew quiet. The lady whom Shira's mother worked for at the big house had come to see them. They were all very frightened even though she smiled at them. She opened a cloth and took out two gold earrings that she gave to Shira's mother. She said, 'I know you have always admired these even though you never said anything. You have always worked hard for me and I want you to have them. You can wear them, or they might come in handy some day because they are very valuable. You might need to sell them for food or even to save your life.'

"Shira's mother stood there silently looking at the earrings. Then she said, 'I cannot accept them. I am sorry. I cannot accept them.' Shira could tell by the way her mother looked that she was angry. It was as if this woman were trying to pay her for all the years of hard work as a slave, and there was no way of ever repaying her for that!

"The lady from the house must have understood, because she said, 'I know that this does not repay you for all these years you have worked for me. There is no way I can give that back to you. The gold earrings are a small way to show you how sorry I am that I have taken advantage of you all these years. I now know that the God of Israel is the Lord of the world, just as Moses says. Pharaoh is only a human king, like others. He thinks he is a god, but he isn't.' When Shira's mother heard this, she accepted the gifts. She knew the lady was truly sorry.

"They left Egypt, and a few months later they were standing at the foot of Mount Sinai. Moses was up on the mountain receiving the commandments from God. Many people got tired of waiting for him. Some thought he had disappeared. Some thought he had died. Some said he just didn't want to lead the people any more and left. Some said God had detained him for some reason. They demanded that Aaron build an idol. The people said that they had no way to speak to God now that Moses was gone, so they said they had to build an idol to guide them. Aaron didn't want to do it, but the people demanded that he make the idol. So Aaron told them to bring their gold earrings to make the idol. Shira's mother refused. She said that God brought them out of Egypt and God would help them now. There was no way an idol could help them.

"When Shira's mother was old, she gave the earrings to Shira, and later, when Shira was old, she gave them to her children. As each generation passed them on to the next, the story was told: 'These came from the time when our family were slaves in Egypt. Never sell them and never give them up. They remind us of our suffering; they remind us how important it is to be free; they remind us of how God protected us and brought us out of Egypt.'

"Hundreds of years went by and still our family kept these earrings. When the Temple in Jerusalem was destroyed, they carried them into exile away from the land of Israel. The family suffered terribly, but no one even thought to sell the earrings.

"Now," said the old woman as she rocked in her chair, "I will tell you how it is that we have only one earring today."

"Long after the Temple was destroyed, our family lived in a little town which had no Torah scroll. The leaders in the town asked everyone to give something to help pay for a Torah scroll. All the people were poor but they gave what they could. Still there was not enough money."

"Finally my great great grandmother, who had the earrings, called the family together and said, 'We have kept these earrings all these centuries in order to remind us that our family were slaves in Egypt and that God freed us. I think we should give one earring to help pay for the Torah scroll, since it tells the story not only of our family but of all the families of the Exodus. We will still have one earring in our family to remind us of our past.' Everyone was very quiet. It was hard to imagine that even one gold earring, which had come all the way from Egypt, across all these centuries, would be sold. But everyone agreed.

"That is how the town got its Torah scroll and that is why there is just one earring left from the Exodus from Egypt."

Values

When we remember our past, we learn about our ancestors: who they were, what they did, and what they taught us. By remembering what came before us, we can understand how our world came to be the way it is. When we remember the past, we can learn important lessons from the wise people who came before us.

Questions for Discussion

Does your family have an object that has been in your family for many, many years? What is it? Why does your family keep it?

Why did Shira and her family keep the earrings for so many years?

Do you think Shira was right not to give an earring to make a golden calf?

Do you think many, many years later it was correct to use one of the earrings to buy a Torah scroll?

Story-Telling Props and Tips

• one big gold earring (a piece of costume jewelry or an earring made out of gold foil paper)

The story may be told as if the teller is a descendent of Shira and her family. Therefore the story can be told as, "our family … we … my great, great grandmother called the family together," and so on.

16

MIRIAM LEADS THE DANCING

BESHALLAḤ, Exodus 13:17—17:16

When Moses was still living in the Pharaoh's palace, one day he saw an Egyptian beating an Israelite slave. Moses was so upset by this sight that he hit the Egyptian and killed him. After that, Moses had to run away, but his sister, Miriam, stayed behind with the Israelites in Egypt. Later on, when the people were free and Israel had passed through the sea, Miriam, who is called a prophetess, led the women in dancing and singing. In this story we learn why she led the singing and dancing and why she is considered a prophetess.

Then Miriam the prophetess, Aaron's sister, took a tambourine in her hand, and all the women went out after her in dance with tambourines. (Exodus 15:20)

After the Israelite slaves heard that Moses had struck an Egyptian, the people talked excitedly about how they would soon be freed. But the Egyptians also knew what Moses had done, so Moses had to flee. The people's mood changed from hope and excitement about freedom to dark despair.

Moses' sister, Miriam, walked along the alleys of the Israelite settlement and looked at the faces of the people. No one smiled. Their faces were full of worry. She thought that this was no way for God's people to feel. She knew she had to do something to encourage them, to give them hope, to help them feel better, and to help them not be so sad. So she took her tambourine, stood on a rock in the middle of the camp, and started to play and sing. Soon a crowd gathered. A few people smiled and some tapped their toes. Miriam began to dance and others joined her. She led them round and round in a circle and sang songs of freedom and songs of praise to God. The people smiled and laughed. She could see how important it was for them to know some joy. She wanted to show them that joy and happiness are ways to draw close to God and that they should never give up hope.

Every day she went out in the camp and found a spot on a hill, called the people together, and told them that she was sure Moses had not just run away, but that he would return. She reminded them that they were God's people and that God would free them, but there would be an important purpose to their freedom. She reminded them that they had to be honest, be kind, and care for one another. Otherwise the freedom they hoped for wouldn't have any value.

As the days and weeks went by and freedom didn't come, some people stopped listening to her. Most of them suffered so much as slaves in Egypt that they were concerned only with getting enough to eat and surviving another day. One man wearing a tattered shirt with no sandals on his feet called out, "You are supposed to be a prophet, so tell us when God will free us. Tell us what is in the future." She calmly explained that prophets don't predict what will happen in the future; prophets speak about what God wants. A woman with a small child yelled back at her, "Get us food, that's what we want, not a lot of talk. Tell God what we want." Miriam assured her, "You will be free. God has promised it."

Most of the people did understand that it would take time before they could be free. Larger and larger crowds of Israelite slaves came to listen to her.

It didn't take long for the Egyptians to find out that Miriam was telling the people that they would soon be free. Of course, the Egyptians didn't like that. They were afraid that she would stir up the people who would then revolt, so they planned to capture Miriam and put her in jail. Miriam always kept an eye out for Egyptian soldiers. One day she got up to speak and, after she had sung a song and told the people that God would free them, she noticed Egyptian soldiers coming toward her. She yelled to everyone to hide, and she escaped down an alleyway. The Egyptians searched but didn't find her.

Another time the Egyptian soldiers dressed up as slaves and joined the crowd where Miriam was speaking. But Miriam expected them to try something like that, so she had her friends watching out for anyone they did not recognize. When the friends saw the Egyptians, they immediately warned Miriam. All of her friends surrounded her, and put different clothes on her; then Miriam just walked away as if she were just another slave.

All the time that Moses was away, Miriam sang and danced with the people to keep up their spirits.

When it came time for the people to leave Egypt, Miriam led them out, dancing and singing. They called her a prophetess because she continued to speak to them of God.

Values

Despite the fact that Miriam suffered along with the rest of the Israelite slaves, she never forgot that God cares about us and wants us to be good and kind people. Even when we are unhappy, it is very important to remember God's concern for us and for how we behave. Miriam also taught us the importance of trying to find some joy even in hard times.

Questions to Discuss

Why did Miriam dance and sing with the people?

What can you do to cheer up people when they are sad or discouraged?

Story-Telling Props and Tips

Play the tambourine and sing a joyful song as part of the story. Or prepare the children to sing and dance to the beat of a tambourine.

17

MOSES AND
THE WISE MAN

YITRO, Exodus 18:1—20:23

After Moses ran away from Egypt, he lived in Midian with a man who would become his father-in-law, Jethro. (He is also called Reuel earlier in the Book of Exodus.) During that time God spoke to Moses out of a burning bush and told him to lead the people out of Egypt. But Moses was afraid he would fail. He was unsure of how he could lead the people out of Egypt as God had commanded him. This story tells how Jethro helped him and it explains why Moses hugged and kissed Jethro when they were reunited after the people were freed from Egypt.

Moses went to meet his father-in-law; he bowed low and kissed him...You shall seek out...able men who fear God, trustworthy men...and let them [serve as] judge[s]... Honor your father and mother. (Exodus 18:7,21–22; 20:12)

After Moses had led the people of Israel out of Egypt, his father-in-law, Jethro, came to see him. Moses bowed to him and kissed him because he wanted to honor him and because Moses loved Jethro very much.

They first met years before when Moses had fled from Egypt. Moses had come to a well. There he chased away some men who wouldn't let Jethro's daughters draw water for their flocks. Jethro had greeted Moses warmly and invited him to eat. Moses was very grateful for Jethro's hospitality. He stayed and helped tend the sheep. In time Moses married Jethro's daughter, Zipporah, and they had two sons.

One day when Moses was tending the sheep, he noticed a burning bush. God spoke to Moses from the bush and told him that he must lead the people of Israel out of Egypt. Moses didn't think he could do it. He was afraid of what would happen to him, and he was also afraid of what would happen to the people if he failed. He knew that he had to do what God asked him, but he was very frightened. After thinking about it for many days, he decided to talk it over with Jethro. Jethro told Moses that the God of Israel was wise and powerful and that he would free the people. Moses felt better but still didn't know how he would free them.

That night Jethro woke Moses and told him to come with him into the desert night. Jethro said that he was going to teach him many important things. Since Moses knew Jethro was one of the wisest men in Midian, he was anxious to learn from Jethro. Stars filled the sky, and Jethro kept looking up because the sky showed him where to go. Finally they reached a cave. Jethro said, "I will teach you how to travel at night. You will never get lost, yet no one will be able to find you in the dark. All you have to do is read the sky and it will show you the way."

Moses thanked Jethro but he was still afraid. "You have shown me how to find my way, but I still don't know how to convince Pharaoh to let the people go." Jethro reassured him that God would protect him and free the Jewish people from Egypt.

The next night Jethro again awakened Moses and took him to the cave. He said, "You will need a way to impress Pharaoh when you first meet him." Then he gave Moses another gift. Jethro held out his staff, which looked like an ordinary staff that shepherds carry. Then Jethro threw it on the ground. It turned into a snake. Jethro then picked it up and it stiffened and turned back into a staff. Moses was amazed. Jethro gave the staff to Moses and showed him how to turn it into a snake and then back into a staff.

Moses again thanked Jethro but asked, "If Pharaoh will let them go, I still don't know how I will lead them. How will I find food and water for them? How will I settle the disagreements they are sure to have?"

Jethro was a wise man who knew much more than how to do tricks. He told Moses that God would provide the food and water that the people would need but that it would be up to Moses to settle their arguments. He told Moses to appoint wise and fair judges who could make peace between the people so that Moses would need to settle only the major disputes.

The next day Moses was ready to leave for Egypt. He told Jethro that he was still afraid. He was afraid of Pharaoh and he was afraid he could not help his people. Moses knew he would miss Jethro and his wife and children. Jethro gave him encouragement and also gave him still another gift. It was a star with the word *shalom* on it. He told Moses to trust that God would protect him and free the people, and he reassured Moses that his family loved him and looked forward to his return. He told Moses always to carry the star so that when he was lonely he could look at it and remember the love of his family and feel the peace of shalom.

That is why Moses loved and honored Jethro and that is why he bowed to him and kissed him when they were reunited after the Exodus.

Values

Jethro saw that Moses was very frightened, so he helped him. Jethro knew that the task God had given to Moses was very important and that God would help, but Moses also had to learn some valuable lessons before he could begin to help his people. We too are sometimes frightened when we have something important to do, but, like Moses, we can understand that God will help us and that there are things others can help us learn. Moses also showed how important it is to show respect for parents, teachers, and others who help us in our lives.

Questions to Discuss

Have you ever wanted to do something but been afraid to do it?

Did anyone teach you something that made you less afraid? How did you thank the person who helped you?

Story-Telling Props and Tips

- food
- decorated staff
- cardboard six-pointed star with *shalom* on it

18

SHULAMIT THE WITNESS

MISHPATIM, Exodus 21:1—24:18

Once God freed the Israelites from Egypt, they needed laws and values to guide them. After the Ten Commandments were presented to the Israelites, many more laws were also given. Among those laws is one that says we should tell the truth when we see wrongdoing. This is a story about Shulamit, a woman who struggled with this law.

You shall not utter a false report; put not your hand with the wicked to be an unrighteous witness. You shall not follow a multitude to do evil. (Exodus 23:1-2)

Shulamit was walking home from work late one night. The streets were dark. She could hear dogs barking from behind fences. Two cats were fighting in an alley. As she turned a corner, she saw two men robbing a third man. Quickly Shulamit ducked into a doorway and held her breath. She could feel her heart beating underneath her coat. Slowly she peeked out to see what was happening. One of the robbers was someone she recognized. It was a man named Bavasi, who was known to be a thief and who was very cruel. She could not see whom they were robbing, but she knew she had to get away from there fast. If Bavasi knew that she had seen the robbery, he would come after her and beat her up to keep her quiet. At the same time she was ashamed that she could not help the man they robbed. "But," she thought, "what could I do? There were two of them and they were very strong and they had clubs. How could I have chased them away?"

Shulamit quickly turned around and went back the way she came. She was very frightened. Just as she turned another corner and thought she had gotten away, she ran into Bavasi.

"Don't you go home the other way?" Bavasi asked.

"Well I forgot something at work," stammered Shulamit, who noticed the bag of things Bavasi had stolen.

"You saw us back there, didn't you?"

Shulamit said, "I didn't see anything." Bavasi didn't believe her. He said, "If anyone asks where you were tonight, say you were with me. Aren't you with me now? You can tell the truth and they will believe you because everybody knows you tell the truth. But if you tell what you saw, you will get this!" And Bavasi shook his fist at her.

So Shulamit went on her way, feeling very troubled. She was enraged at Bavasi for robbing that man, but she was terrified that Bavasi would beat her up. Shulamit decided not to say anything unless she was asked. The next day she <u>was</u> asked. "Did you hear," said her friend, "someone was beaten and robbed last night—it was near where you walk home—did you see anything?" How could she lie to her friend? So she told him what happened. Shulamit's friend asked if she saw who it was and Shulamit told her that she didn't know. He said, "Keep quiet or they will come after you." So Shulamit didn't tell anyone.

In a few days, officers from the village guard came by. They wanted to know if she had seen anything. She told them she had walked home just as she always did. They asked her about Bavasi. She said she walked part of the way with him. The officers were satisfied. She was relieved but she felt like a coward. How could she protect Bavasi? Yet she knew that if she spoke up she would be beaten, either by Bavasi or by one of his men.

Two days later she heard that it was her dear friend Lazer who was robbed. How could she not come forward for her friend? How could she look her friend in the eye again if she didn't tell what she saw? But how could she protect herself?

Shulamit went to see Rabbi Moshe. She told the rabbi the whole story and asked what she should do. The rabbi said, "I understand that you are afraid, but for a witness to lie is a serious wrong, a more serious wrong than a simple lie. You should speak up, but not only because this happened to your friend—you should speak up for anyone. This is what you must do. You must go to the village guard and tell them what happened. Tell them the whole truth. Tell them that you are afraid because Bavasi threatened you. Tell the village guard you want it known that you were a witness to what Bavasi did."

"But," said Shulamit, "Bavasi will be sure to come after me."

"That is the idea. Let him come with all his men and let the village guard be there to catch them all."

That is what Shulamit did and that is how the village guard stopped Bavasi from robbing and hurting more people. That is how Shulamit learned how important it is to be a truthful witness.

Values

Certainly we should tell the truth about what we see, even though doing so may be hard. Just living every day means that we witness many things. If we are a witness, directly or indirectly, to a wrong, an injustice, or a hurt, we should try to right the wrong, correct the injustice, or heal the hurt.

Questions to Discuss

Why did Shulamit go to the rabbi?

Have you ever seen someone do something wrong to another person? Were you afraid to tell someone about it? What did you finally decide to do?

Story-Telling Props and Tips

• Bavasi's club
• bag with stolen property
• police hat or badge
• hat, shawl, or other item Shulamit might have worn

19

THREE FRIENDS

TERUMAH, Exodus 25:1—27:19

When the people of Israel were in Egypt, they were slaves to
Pharaoh, who the Egyptians thought of as a god. When they
finally left Egypt, they built the Tabernacle, a portable sanctuary where they could worship the true God. This story is
about three friends who escaped from Egyptian slavery to
help Moses free the people and then finally to build and carry
the Tabernacle.

***And let them make Me a sanctuary that I may dwell
among them.*** (Exodus 25:8)

    Long ago when the people of Israel were slaves in Egypt, there
were three friends: Zohar, Carmi, and Tamara. They were very different
from each other. Zohar was huge. He was almost seven feet tall and was
one of the strongest people in all Egypt. Then there was Carmi, who told
stories, and Tamara, who sang beautiful songs. They were such good
friends that they would have given their lives for each other.
    They had to work in the hot sun all day and they had little to eat.
Their job was cutting huge stones and moving them onto rollers, where
the buildings in honor of Pharaoh were being built. The work was very
hard. Even worse than the work itself was the thought that they were
building a tomb for Pharaoh, who was considered to be a god by the
Egyptians.

These three friends had spoken many times of how they might help their people. They heard that the Egyptian prince, Moses, had killed an Egyptian and had run away into the desert. There were rumors that Moses was plotting to free them. The friends spoke about trying to go to find him. Then something happened that made them try to escape from Egypt.

One day Carmi got caught in one of the ropes that pulled the stones, and broke his arm. Because he couldn't work, an Egyptian guard beat him with a club. Zohar wanted to save his friend but there were other guards nearby with swords, and other guards with bows and arrows stood on the high walls. He knew that if he tried to help, the Egyptians would kill both of them. He could only stand and watch, feeling helpless and full of rage. All of a sudden there was a loud whistle and all the guards ran in another direction. Some Hebrews in another area must have realized what was happening and made a commotion to distract the guards. That gave Zohar and Tamara time to carry Carmi away so they could take care of him.

They put a splint on Carmi's arm and bandaged his wounds from the beating. In a week Carmi felt stronger, but he couldn't work and the guards were sure to come back for him. Zohar and Tamara knew they couldn't hide him much longer and that they would have to escape soon. It would be very dangerous. The walls were closely guarded and they would be killed if they were caught. Even if they escaped, where would they go?

The next night there was a storm. It rained very hard and there was no moon. This was the perfect night for the escape, because it would be difficult for the guards to see them.

The three friends hid near the wall and started digging. Finally, after a whole night of digging, they managed to sneak under the wall and went out into the desert. They had very little food and water, and after a day or two they had nothing left. They didn't even know where they should go. All they knew was that they had to find Moses, to see if he was going to lead the people and to ask if they could help him.

On the fourth day, they saw two clouds of dust. One moved very fast. It was Egyptian soldiers looking for them. The other was from a flock of sheep. As the soldiers were coming closer, the shepherd drove his flocks between them and the friends. The shepherd told them to pretend that they were shepherds with him so that when the soldiers came near they would just look around and then go on their way.

This shepherd was very kind. He gave them food and water. The friends traveled with him and his flocks for a few days. They asked him about Moses, but he just shrugged his shoulders. They noticed that he spoke Egyptian, that he stuttered, and that when they spoke Hebrew among themselves he listened very carefully as if he understood them. They also noticed that he treated the lambs very kindly. When one of the lambs got tired, he would carry it. He also spoke very softly to the lambs and they really seemed to love him.

Finally one day the shepherd spoke to them in Hebrew and admitted to them that he was Moses. He told them that he wanted to be sure of who they really were before he told them who he was. Moses told them that God had promised to help the people and that he and his brother, Aaron, would soon speak to Pharaoh. Moses told the friends that he was afraid the Israelite people would not follow him. The friends could help by speaking to the Israelites and giving them the courage to follow Moses and Aaron out of Egypt.

The friends snuck back into the Israelite camp and told the people they had spoken to Moses. The Exodus would soon begin!

When the time of the Exodus came, the three friends helped however they could. They carried lambs, children, and old people who were too weak to walk. They joyously helped to build and then carry the Tabernacle, which was where the people worshiped God in the desert. Even though it was very heavy and the sun was very hot, they worked with joy. Tamara led them in songs, Carmi told stories, and Zohar stood straighter and taller than ever.

When it came time to set up the portable sanctuary, they led the singing and dancing. Now they were free and could work hard for their people and for God, instead of as slaves for a man who pretended to be a god.

Values

In this passage God tells the people to "build Me a house that I may dwell among them." In Egypt, Israel had to build the house of a person who pretended to be God. Now they were free and could build a house where they would worship God. It would be a place where they would feel God's presence. We in our time can use our freedom to turn away from the idols of our day, to worship God, and to build a world in which God's presence can be felt.

Questions to Discuss

Why were the three friends so happy to build the Tabernacle in the desert?

Do you think people ever worship idols today?
What might those idols be?

Story-Telling Props and Tips

• a hat for each of the friends, Moses, and an Egyptian
• stuffed lamb for Moses to hold
• spear for Egyptian

20

AARON'S SONS WANT
SPECIAL CLOTHES

TETZAVEH, Exodus 27:20—30:10

After the Tabernacle was built, God gave directions on making special clothes for the priests to wear. This is a story
about how the sons of Aaron misunderstood the purpose of
those clothes and how they learned what they really mean.

*[God said to Moses,] "You shall bring forward your
brother Aaron, with his sons...to serve Me as priests.
Make holy garments...for splendor and beauty."*
(Exodus 28:1-2)

God said that the priests should wear holy garments for "splendor
and beauty." Aaron the High Priest had four sons: Nadab, Abihu, Elazar,
and Itamar. As soon as they heard about the special clothes, each one
imagined how he would look. Each thought that these clothes would
make him very, very important.

Nadab, the oldest son, put on the *ephod*—the short coat. He
marched around in front of his friends as if to say, "I have something you
don't have." He felt that he was better than they were because he had
this ephod.

Abihu, Aaron's second son, put on the *hoshen*—breastplate—with
twelve jewels, one for each of the twelve tribes. He paraded around as
though he were very important, as if to say, "Look at me. Aren't I wonderful because I have this breastplate?" He too felt that he was better
than anyone else.

Elazar, Aaron's third son, put on the long blue robe. He walked out in front of his friends and hoped that they would envy him. He knew that only the priestly family of Aaron could wear these clothes, and he wanted everyone else to know how important he was.

Itamar, the youngest son, put on the special headdress with a gold plate on the front. He looked at himself and thought he looked splendid, but his smile soon turned into a frown. He wanted to be the only one with such beautiful clothes, or at least he wanted more beautiful clothes than his brothers had. He wanted his brothers to envy him. He had always gotten hand-me-down clothes from his brothers. Now he wanted to be the only one with such beautiful clothes. So Itamar did a terrible thing. He took his brothers' special clothes and hid them. Then he pretended that he didn't know anything about the missing clothes.

Their father, Aaron, had seen what his sons were doing. He saw how they walked around showing off their clothes, and he was very upset. Now that the clothes of three of the brothers had disappeared, he was even more concerned. These were not just ordinary clothes. They were the clothes that God had commanded them to make for the priests in the Temple.

There was quite an uproar when the brothers realized that the clothes were missing. Everyone in the family looked all over the camp. They looked under the mattresses, in their wagons, and everywhere else they could think of. Of course, everyone thought it was strange that only Itamar still had his special clothes, but he didn't care. Now that he was the only one of the brothers who had special clothes, they would envy him. They would wish that they had the clothes too.

Aaron posted a reward: anyone who returned the clothes would be given seven pieces of silver—no questions asked. But no clothes were found. This search went on for a week, for two weeks. Still no clothes. Nadab, Abihu, and Eleazar moped around all day. Finally they came to Itamar. They were sure he knew something about the missing clothes. After all, he still had his own clothes. They demanded that he tell them what happened. Itamar denied knowing anything about them.

Finally Aaron came to Itamar and asked him what happened. Now Itamar could lie to his brothers, but he would never lie to his father. So he confessed. He said he had taken the clothes because his brothers were always getting more than he was; everything always seemed to go well for them; why should he, as the youngest, always come last; why shouldn't he have something special that they didn't have, just this once?

The three brothers were relieved that their clothes were found, but Aaron wouldn't return them right away. He even took Itamar's clothes away from him. He told each of them that they had to earn the right to wear those clothes. They each had to do a mitzvah, a holy deed, to help the community. He told Nadab to help the elderly to carry their things. He told Abihu to care for and play with the sick children. He told Eleazar to clean up the camp. And he told Itamar to stand guard against wild animals attacking the camp during the night.

The brothers looked at one another. They should do those lowly tasks? Weren't there others who could do these things? They, the children of Aaron the priest, the ones who had those beautiful special clothes? They didn't understand why their father was telling them to do this. Nadab, Abihu, and Elazar were especially angry, because it was their clothes that had been stolen and now it looked like they were being punished.

Each of the brothers began his task. They each worked hard at what he was doing. Each of them learned about the different things needed to keep the community running. They each heard stories of how hard life was for some other people. And soon they got involved in helping them.

When Aaron saw how their attitudes had changed, he called them together and said, "Wearing the holy garments is a privilege. When it is said that they are for 'splendor and beauty,' that doesn't mean they are to make you full of splendor and beauty. All that walking around being so proud of yourself and wanting everyone to think you are so special was wrong. What makes you special is not the clothes that you wear, but the kind of person you are. What 'splendor and beauty' means is that the clothes are to make the worship of God full of 'splendor and beauty.' The purpose is to bring you and the people closer to God. The purpose is to make the worship of God more beautiful."

Then Aaron gave them back their special clothes. He told them they had now earned them. Each brother took the clothes and put them away. Now they used them only when they went into the holy Temple. The rest of the time they wore ordinary clothes and worked to help others.

Values

Aaron explained that the special priestly clothes are to make the worship of God full of "splendor and beauty." Jews try to make the synagogue a beautiful place. We try to buy beautiful Kiddush cups and candle sticks for our homes and synagogues. None of this is to make us feel that we are better than other people are, or to make us feel important. All of these things are part of what is called *hiddur mitzvah*—to make the doing of a mitzvah more beautiful. It is one way of doing the mitzvah with care, love, and enthusiasm. Their purpose is not to show off to others, but to have these beautiful things inspire us to feel closer to God.

For Roman Catholics, the beautification of churches is to honor God and to show God's beauty. Being attentive to the decor of the church is a way of being attentive to God. The vestments worn by the priest (alb, stole, and chasuble) are symbolic of the priest's baptism, role, and the time of the year.

For many Protestants, the purpose of artistic creation in churches is to awaken God's presence in the worshiper.

Questions to Discuss

Is your synagogue or church a nice place?
Why do the people there try to make it look nice,
and why do they try to keep it clean?

Story-Telling Props and Tips

Make simple fabric replicas of the priests' clothing, or even use enlarged drawings, which can be copied from books: *ephod* with two jewels, *hoshen* with twelve jewels, long robe with bells, headdress with gold plate for God's name.

As the story is told, children can be called up to hold the picture or wear part of the clothing. The clothes can be taken away and then old work hats can be given to them to show they are going to work with the poor.

For an illustration of the priests' clothing see *Encyclopaedia Judaica*, XIII:1066.

21

BEZALEL MAKES BEAUTIFUL THINGS

KI TISSA, Exodus 30:11—34:35

In this Torah portion, which describes the building of the Tabernacle, God tells Moses to call upon Bezalel to make the many beautiful things that would be used there. This story tells about Bezalel when he was a child and explains why God chose him to do this important work.

See I have singled out by name Bezalel...and I have filled him with the spirit of God, in wisdom, and in understanding, and in knowledge, and in all manner of workmanship to devise skillful works...in gold... silver and...brass. (Exodus 31:2-4)

Bezalel was a very unusual little boy. He liked to make things—not just ordinary things, but fantastic things. And he seemed to make them from practically nothing. He would pick up bits of string, a piece of cloth, a little wire, some paint. He could make toys, unusual birds, hanging things, even jewelry. He loved the feel of the pen on the paper, the texture of fabric, or the clay in his hands.

Mostly he made things to give to other people. At first he gave the things he made to his parents and to his brother and sister. It gave him a good feeling to see how much they enjoyed his gifts. Sometimes he gave them a gift for a birthday or because they did something for him or because he was sorry about something he had done. Sometimes he made them a gift just because he loved them. He made just the right gift for each person. It seemed as if Bezalel could talk to people through the things he made. When he gave them the gifts, they would thank him and he could see the joy in their eyes. Sometimes they would give him a hug and ask him how he made the gift and why he painted it such and such a color and so on. Usually he would say something very short like, "I like the way it looks," or "My heart told me to do it that way."

Bezalel was able to express what was in his heart through the things he made with his hands. Words were not necessary.

Another unusual thing about Bezalel was that he didn't say much. He could speak, but he was so quiet that his parents sometimes wondered if he really knew how to speak. His teachers complained that he almost never said anything.

One of Bezalel's friends, Channah, became very sick. She had to stay in bed for many weeks. Bezalel got busy making games for her to play with and pretty pictures to look at. When she returned to school, she told everyone how much all their good wishes meant to her and then said, "I especially want to thank Bezalel. I loved playing the games he made and looking at the pretty pictures. Even if I felt weak, I could look at the things he made and feel better." After class the teacher called Bezalel over and told him, "You have shown that you know how to speak with your heart and your mind. You do it by making things for people. I don't have to hear you say anything to know what is in your heart. I can see it by what you make."

There were times when Bezalel used words. That was when he prayed. He knew how to read the prayerbook and he also prayed with his own words. As Bezalel got older, words didn't seem to be the right way to show how grateful he was to God. God made a beautiful world for him and he wondered about making a gift for God.

But how could he make something for God? God didn't need anything. God only wanted people to care about one another. Bezalel was sitting under the shade of a tree and thinking about what kind of gift would bring people closer together. He wondered what kind of gift he could make for God that would show a little of the beauty God had given to him.

God felt Bezalel's love and told Moses to call upon Bezalel to create beautiful things for the Temple. God wanted Moses to tell the people of Israel all about Bezalel: "See I have called Bezalel by name and filled him with the spirit of God, in wisdom, in understanding and in knowledge and in all kinds of workmanship."

This is how Bezalel was chosen to build the portable sanctuary that brought the people of Israel closer to one another and to God. This is how Bezalel got to make something beautiful for God and gave God a gift.

Values

There are many different ways of showing love and concern for others, and each of us has our own special way of expressing our feelings to others. Some use words, but others like Bezalel, can make things. But no matter how we express ourselves, it is important to show others that we care about them. It is also important to show God how grateful we are for all that God has done for us.

Questions to Discuss

Do you like to make things? What kinds of things do you make?
....
Do you ever make things and give them to people?
Why? How does it make you feel?
....
What kind of a gift would you make for God?
....

Story-Telling Props and Tips

- Before telling the story ask the children to bring in toys, jewelry, or other things that they have made.
- Gather some children's artwork and show it during the story.

22

GOD'S GARDEN

VAYAKHEL-PEKUDEI, Exodus 35:1—40:38

The Bible gives many instructions on how to build the Tabernacle. It says that blue, purple, and crimson should be used. We may wonder why those colors were required. This story tells about a girl named Shoshana who loved God and the flowers God created. It will also tell us why blue, purple, and crimson were used in decorating the Tabernacle.

Take from among you gifts for God; everyone whose heart so moves him shall bring them—gifts for God... blue, purple and crimson. (Exodus 35:5-6)

Of the blue, purple and crimson yarns they made the vestments. (Exodus 39:1)

There was once a young girl named Shoshana. Every day she would disappear for a while. No one could find her. She was very tall for her age, but she was still young, and her family worried about her. No one knew that she picked flowers from the nearby hills and, when no one was looking, left them at the place where they were building the Tabernacle. There were almond blossoms, big fig leaves, and red and blue flowers whose names she didn't know.

Her father always told her, "Don't go wandering off. There are wild animals out in the desert. And you could get lost."

But Shoshana was stubborn and went anyway. One time she did get lost, and she spent the night curled up shivering next to a tree. This time her mother was frantic. After she was found, her father said, "You're grounded! You can't go out again for two weeks."

But after the two weeks were over she went off again. This time she ran into a leopard. He was coming down a slope, hissing at her. Shoshana kept a steady eye on him and picked up a broken branch to protect herself. He came closer. She was very frightened and wanted to try to run away, but she knew she could never outrun a leopard. So she stood there with the branch in her hand staring right into his eyes, trying not to look afraid. Slowly the leopard backed off and went away.

Shoshana continued to pick flowers and bring bouquets to the place where the Tabernacle was being built. She always left them when no one was looking, so the priests never knew where the flowers came from. One afternoon as she was leaving the flowers, one of the priests caught her. "What are you doing here?" he demanded. "Don't you know this is where the Tabernacle will be? Go home to your family."

She explained that she came to leave the flowers. He tried to chase her away but she wouldn't go. Finally he called the High Priest, who asked her, "What are you doing?"

"I'm bringing flowers for the new Tabernacle."

"Why?" he demanded. "We usually don't have flowers here."

Shoshana replied, "I want to bring God's garden here into God's house."

The priest smiled and blessed her.

That is why the Tabernacle was created with blue, purple, and crimson yarns—because these are the colors of the flowers of God's garden.

Values

When this passage in Exodus says that each person whose heart moves him or her shall bring gifts, it means all of us, young and old, rich and poor. Each person can contribute in his or her own way to the worship of God. Each of us can bring our own special gifts to making God's world a better place. Each of us can show our thankfulness to God in our own special way.

Questions to Discuss

What do you especially like to do?

Do you collect anything? Is there a way that you could use the things you like to do or collect to help others or to show God how thankful you are for what you have?

Story-Telling Props and Tips

- compass (so she doesn't get lost again!)
- stick
- flowers
- big leaves
- blue, purple, and crimson yarns

23

PENINA'S GARDEN

VAYIKRA, Leviticus 1:1—5:26

As we begin the Book of Leviticus, we enter the world of the animal sacrifices and offerings of fruit, grain, and oil. This was the way the Jewish people used to worship God. One of the offerings was made up of the first fruits of the season, vegetables and grain that they grew. This story tells about a little girl who, long after the Temple was destroyed, grew corn and wanted to find a way to thank God for the wonderful gift of crops.

When you bring a meal offering of first fruits to Adonai, bring...grain. (Leviticus 2:14)

When Penina was ten, her mother and father set aside a part of their garden just for her. She always liked to work in the family garden, and she was very excited about having her own section. Now she could decide what she wanted to plant. She planted corn, which she loved to eat, and some pink petunias, which she thought were really cute.

In the spring, when the ground was warm, Penina made little holes in the ground and put in corn seeds. Then she made a little groove in the earth and sprinkled the petunia seeds in a row. She filled her watering can and sprinkled all the places where she had planted seeds. She waited. The next morning she looked out—nothing had happened. She waited a week and still nothing grew. She watered the ground every few days and waited. A few days later she finally noticed something green sprouting. Every day she checked on the little sprout. Over the next two days it grew even bigger. It didn't look like corn or petunias. She decided it was a weed and pulled it out. Three days after that the petunias came up. They looked like little green shoots coming up in a row. She watered them and continued to watch. Then the corn came up. It looked like rolled-up paper that kept getting higher and higher. Then one day she noticed that some of the leaves on the corn had big chunks taken out of them. Something was eating her corn! She was furious. How dare they. She got some soapy water and sprayed the leaves. The next day the leaves looked fine.

The corn soon grew taller than Penina. She got a ladder and climbed up to look at it. She saw that brown tassels were beginning to form. They looked like silk thread. Of course she didn't need the ladder for the petunias. She could look right at their beautiful floppy pink petals. She picked some to put in her room. She knew that if she picked them, more flowers would grow, and that is exactly what happened. It was amazing. The corn seeds knew to grow into corn and the petunias knew to grow into pink petunias. Not only that, but when she picked petunias, the plants knew that they should make more pink petunia flowers. Wonderful!

Penina knew that the best part was yet to come: ears of corn. After several weeks she saw the ears of corn bulging from the stalks, and when they were ready, she picked the first ear. It was beautiful. It had a deep green cover with soft white leaves underneath and even softer strands of silk underneath that. How well it was wrapped—carefully, securely, and beautifully. It almost looked as if it were gift wrapped, she thought. Well if it was gift wrapped, then it was a gift and she needed to say thank you. But to whom? She had grown it. Should she thank herself? She knew she had worked hard, but she knew that she didn't make the seed, or the soft, warm ground, or the water. She only helped it along.

She decided that she should thank God. But how? She had heard how the people of Israel would bring the first fruits as an offering to the Temple. But there was no Temple now. What should she do? How could she tell God that she was grateful for the corn. She decided that she could thank God by sharing her gift with those who didn't have enough to eat, and so she took a basket, filled it with the most beautiful ears of corn, and brought it to the soup kitchen in her village.

Values

Everything we have comes partly from our own efforts but mostly from what God has given us. Like Penina, we too want to thank God for the gifts of what we have. We thank God when we say a blessing before or after we eat. We also show our appreciation to God by doing what God wants us to do: to share the bounty of God's earth with others. We do that by making donations to funds for the hungry and/or by bringing food to a local food pantry.

Questions to Discuss

Do you have a garden? Did you ever plant seeds? What happened?

Can plants grow without any assistance from people?
What can we learn from this?

Story-Telling Props and Tips

- corn seeds
- a watering can
- an ear of corn
- a ladder
- some petunias

Have children act out parts of the story using the props. Popcorn might be made and served afterwards.

Children may be asked to bring in food for the poor.

Provide cups or a tray of soil for planting seeds.

24

THREE PEOPLE, ONE SACRIFICE

TZAV, Leviticus 6:1—8:36

This Torah portion tells how people would bring various offerings to the priests in the ancient Temple, who then placed them on the altar before God. This story tells what happened when three people who had done wrong brought offerings to a wise priest named Eleazer.

This is the ritual of the guilt offering: it is most holy.
(Leviticus 7:1)

It was a bright day in Jerusalem, and Eleazer the priest was thankful for the warm sun after the chilly winter. He washed, prayed, and then studied. Before he went to the Temple, he put money into a box for the poor. On his way to the Temple he visited a sick neighbor. All of these acts were part of his careful preparation for the offering of sacrifices in the Temple. He knew that he had to try to be a good person or the sacrifices would be meaningless.

On this morning Reuven came to offer a goat as a sin offering—that is an offering to God to show how bad he felt for having done wrong. Reuven was a tall, thin man with a purple coat and a round hat. Eleazer asked him what he had done wrong. Reuven told him that he had cheated someone. A man had come into his shop and paid for the best quality barley, but Reuven had given him poor quality barley by mistake. The man never realized he had gotten inferior barley. Eleazer asked Reuven if he had refunded the money or given the man the proper barley. Reuven told him he hadn't. "That's why I am bringing an offering. I don't want God to be angry with me." Eleazer told him to go and give the man back his money. After he did that, he could offer a sacrifice to ask God's forgiveness.

"But," Reuven protested, "I want to bring the sacrifice instead of giving the money back. It would be embarrassing to go to the customer. Word might get around that I can't be trusted. The customer lives far away and it would be inconvenient to get to him. Besides, I don't have much money and I can't afford to repay him. You know, business is business."

Eleazer told him, "The man and everyone else would probably consider you more honest if you repaid the money."

Reuven suggested, "Suppose I give the money to the poor instead of to the customer. Then the people who need it most would be helped."

Eleazer was firm: "First you have to repay the person you cheated, even if you pay him back a little at a time. Only then can you offer a sacrifice to show God how sorry you are."

Reuven left grumbling.

Sara, a tall, thin woman, came to Eleazer. "I am a teacher and I insulted a student in front of the class. I called him stupid, and I feel very bad about doing that. I didn't mean to say anything nasty to him, but I was angry with him for not doing his homework. The words came out before I could stop them, and I want to offer a sin offering."

"Did you apologize to the student?"

"No," said Sara.

"Did you tell the other students in the class that you are sorry?"

"No."

"Then you can't offer a sacrifice. You have to apologize first and then go to the people who heard the insult and tell them that you were wrong. Then you can come back to offer a sacrifice."

"But I can't do that. It would be humiliating to apologize to him in front of the class. Besides, it was partly his fault. He didn't do his homework."

"But you did insult him."

"I'm sorry, I just can't do it. Let me offer the sacrifice."

"No. You can't offer a sacrifice until you speak to the student and the class. Sin offerings are only for when you have already done your best for the person you wronged. Then you can ask God for forgiveness."

"Okay, I'll try, but it won't be easy."

Sara came back a few days later and told Eleazer that she had apologized in front of the class, and not only did the student thank her and say he would be careful about the homework, but, she added, "All the students seem to respect me more!"

Joyfully Eleazer offered the sacrifice to God.

Later that day an old man named Joseph came to Eleazer. He was leaning on a cane. He said, "Many years ago I picked up a piece of wood and hit a man. I hit him hard. In those days I really had a temper and I was very strong. The man fell down and hurt his back. He couldn't work for many months. I ran away to the next town where no one knew me. I started a new life. I had forgotten about the incident until recently when someone did the same thing to my son. He can't work and he has a hard time trying to earn a living. That is why I want to bring a sacrifice. I want God to understand how sorry I feel for what I did."

Eleazer listened carefully and asked, "Have you tried to help the man you hit? Did you pay him for the time he could not work?"

"I looked all over for him and I finally found him. I went to see him and he told me that it took him three months to recover. I saved and paid him for the time he lost at work. The man was very surprised and didn't even want to take the money. He said it happened such a long time ago and he didn't need the money now. But I insisted, and he took the money. Now I want to show God how sorry I am and ask God to forgive me."

For this man, Eleazer offered the sacrifice to God. As he did, the man seemed to look younger. He stood up straighter. He smiled and sang a song of praise to God.

Values

Sometimes we wrong other people, but before we can ask God to forgive us, we must try to make amends to the person we have hurt.

Questions to Discuss

Have you ever hurt anyone's feelings? Did you ever take something, even by mistake, that did not belong to you?

How did you feel about doing those things?
What do you think you can do to set things right with that person?

Why do you think it is also important to tell God that you are sorry
for what you did?

Story-Telling Props and Tips

- box used to collect money for the poor
- flowers or pot for soup for the sick person
- basket or bag of barley
- book a teacher might have
- cane
- piece of wood
- money

25

AARON'S SONS TRY TO FEEL IMPORTANT

SHEMINI, Leviticus 9:1—11:47

This passage tells how two of Aaron's sons did the wrong thing when they offered incense to God. Incense is sweet-smelling spices which are brought as an offering. In this story we learn more about why they acted wrongly and we see that it is important that people who perform the various rituals understand them and appreciate the meaning of what they are doing.

Now Aaron's sons, Nadab and Abihu, each took his fire pan, put fire in it, and laid incense on it; and they offered before Adonai alien fire, which God had not commanded them to do. (Leviticus 10:1)

The sons of Aaron loved to watch as their father went into the Sanctuary. He prepared himself by washing his hands and feet, putting on the special robes, and praying; only then did he offer incense to God.

Two of Aaron's sons, Nadab and Abihu, watched this scene many times. They couldn't wait for the day when they too could offer the incense. They were anxious to do the best for their people, but they often got in their father's way. At Mount Sinai they had even tried to follow Moses up the mountain! Their father saw them just in time and stopped them.

Now as they watched their father prepare and offer the incense, they looked at one another and said, "that looks easy—put incense in pan, add hot coals, shake it to mix them up, and bring the fire pan to the altar." They could do that! They too could be priests; they could be just like their father. Nadab and Abihu decided to try it themselves. They waited until their father was busy teaching others and they put on the sacred clothes. My how grown-up they looked! Of course the sacred robes were too long for them and they tried to hold them up as they walked to the Tent of Meeting. People looked at them and made room for them to pass.

Finally they arrived at the Tent of Meeting, went in, and found where their father kept the incense. They decided that they were clean enough, so they didn't bother washing as their father always did, even when it didn't look like he was dirty. They were so excited about preparing the incense that they didn't stop to study and pray as their father did before he performed the offerings.

Meanwhile a friend of Aaron's saw the boys and ran to tell Aaron. Aaron was horrified that his sons would defile the sacred clothes. He was even more horrified at the possibility that they were not just walking around in the sacred robes but that they would actually try to make an offering. He left his students and ran to the Tent of Meeting to stop his sons.

Meanwhile the boys had already taken the incense and put it in the pans. They had a hard time gathering up the hot coals from the altar. But finally they managed to put the incense in the pan, add coals, and shake it around just as their father had done. Then they brought it over to the altar. They were delighted that they were able to offer the incense. Aaron was just at the entrance of the Tent of Meeting when he smelled the incense. His sons had done a terrible thing; they had used the priesthood, the sacred clothes, and the incense to make themselves feel grown-up like their father. It was too late. Because of what they had done, his sons would never again enter the Tent of Meeting.

Then Aaron called his other sons and told them, "Your brothers have done a terrible thing. I want you to understand that the worship in the Tent of Meeting and the rituals of Jewish life are very beautiful and have deep meaning. It may look easy to prepare the incense offering and the other offerings, and in a way it *is* easy. Anyone can mix incense and hot coals in a pan. But to make it a real offering you have to understand and appreciate what you are doing. That takes years of study and prayer. The purpose of the rituals is to help us feel closer to our people and to

God—not simply to do them. When you are ready to really understand the meaning of what you are doing, it will be a great joy for me to bring you to the Tent of Meeting and allow you to perform the offerings."

Values

The customs, holidays, and rituals of religion help us feel closer to God, to our families, and to our people. In the synagogue, only those who are over the age of 13 are called to the Torah, even though younger children may know how to say the blessings. The reason is that it is important that they be old enough to understand and appreciate the meaning of what they are doing.

This is true not only of Judaism. Many religious traditions require people to be of a certain age or have certain education before they can participate in some of their religious practices.

Questions to Discuss

Do you ever have the chance to say any special prayers at home?

Was someone in your family ever given an honor as part of worship services?

Would you like to have a special honor? Why?

Story-Telling Props and Tips

- a pan where Aaron can pretend to wash
- some articles of "priest's clothing"
- a tin plate that could be the "incense holder"
- some rocks to stand for the hot coals

26

CARE OF THE SICK

TAZRIA-METZORA, Leviticus 12:1—15:33

In the two Torah portions of Tazria and Metzora we are told how the priests brought people who had suffered from the disease of leprosy back into the community. In this story, which takes place long after the people of Israel are settled in the land of Israel, Rafaela helps a sick child feel part of the community. She then uses this passage from the Torah to teach what should be done to help others who are sick.

This shall be the ritual for a leper at the time that he is to be cleansed...After that he may come into the camp.
(Leviticus 14:2,8)

Judith was out playing one day when she began to feel very sick. Her head hurt, her body hurt, she felt hot, she felt cold, and she felt dizzy. She suddenly fell down and couldn't get up. Her friends came over and asked her what was wrong. Her eyes were closed. She didn't answer. When they asked if she could hear them, she mumbled something they couldn't understand. They had never seen her this way. She was always running and playing. Her friends were very frightened and they yelled for help. Almost immediately, several adults came. The adults put Judith on a wagon and pushed her home, with all the children trotting alongside. When they got to Judith's house, her parents carried Judith inside and put her to bed.

For six days Judith lay in bed. She was hot and then cold. Sometimes she opened her eyes and mumbled a little, sometimes she mumbled in her sleep, but mostly she just slept soundly. Everyone was worried that Judith would never get better. But then, on the morning of the seventh day, Judith opened her eyes and asked for water. The next day she asked for food, so they gave her bread and a little cheese. Pretty soon she sat up in bed and was able to speak with people. She could even stand up with a little help. In a few more days she could walk with help.

By now her parents had not worked in two weeks and they were running out of money. They decided it would be safe to leave her alone while they went to work. They put water and food near Judith's bed, told her not to try to walk around, and promised they would be home as soon as they could.

Judith was alone. The first day she counted the tiles on the ceiling. Then she counted the stripes on her blanket. The next day she made up stories and pretended that her bed was a magic carpet. She imagined that she flew to a castle. There she was a brave warrior who went off to battle on her magic carpet and was able to defeat any enemy.

After four days of being alone, Judith ran out of things to do. She heard her friends playing outside and wanted to run and play with them. She remembered that her parents told her she must stay in bed, and that it was dangerous for her to try to walk around by herself. Yet she was feeling a little better. She decided to try to sit up. She felt fine. Then she slowly pushed herself up and stood by the bed. She felt a little shaky at first, but after a few minutes she felt better. She decided to take a step while holding onto the wall. She didn't feel very strong, but she was able to stand and walk a little. She tried walking to the next room. Once there, she sat down for a moment. Soon she felt steady enough to try for the front door. She leaned against walls, a chair, and a table until she reached it. She was tired but she had gotten there on her own! She rested for a moment and then opened the door. It was wonderful. She felt the warm sunshine and breeze on her face. She took a deep breath of fresh air, ran outside, and then collapsed. Again her friends saw her and called for help. Again Judith was brought back into the house. A neighbor ran to get her parents.

Rafaela, another neighbor, helped get Judith into bed and waited until her parents got home. Judith's parents asked her why she had been so foolish. Judith told them that she thought she would be all right. She just wanted to be with her friends. Her parents scolded her and told her not to do that again. But Rafaela had another idea. She explained to them that Judith only wanted to be with her friends, so

Rafaela arranged for people to bring games and puzzles for Judith to play with and for them to come after school to keep Judith company. Rafaela arranged for a neighbor to spend time with Judith in the morning so she wouldn't be alone so much. The teacher came from school to help Judith keep up with her work. Rafaela said this is called *bikkur cholim*—visiting the sick.

Later, when Judith was stronger, she went back to school. Rafaela came to the school to thank the students and the teacher for helping Judith. She said, "People who are sick shouldn't be alone. They are part of our community. They need to be included in what we do. Always remember that it is important to visit the sick and to make them feel that we care about them. That's what the Torah means when it says, 'He may come into the camp'—it means that people who are sick should be included in our lives."

Values

When people are ill, it is important not only to take care of them by making sure they get the medicine they need. We should also visit them, keep them company, let them know that we care about them, cheer them up, and say a prayer with them.

Questions to Discuss

Have you ever been sick and had to stay in bed?
How did you feel about getting visitors and having things to do?

Have you ever visited anyone who was sick?
How do you think your visit made the person feel?

Story-Telling Props and Tips

- a blanket that has a design of items that can be counted
- a small carpet and crown
- games and puzzles

Invite children to bring games and puzzles as gifts for children in shelters for the homeless or in hospitals. Or provide a list of gifts that the children can bring in at a later time.

27

SARA CATCHES A THIEF

AHAREI MOT-KEDOSHIM, Leviticus 16:1—20:27

The overall theme of these passages is the many things the people of Israel should do, and not do, in order to be a holy people. This story deals with a case of stealing and talebearing.

You shall not steal; you shall not deal deceitfully or falsely with one another...You shall not go about as a talebearer. (Leviticus 19:11,16)

In a small village there once lived a little boy named Shimon. He was smaller than the other boys of his age and they often made fun of him because of his size. They also made fun of him because he had freckles, and because he couldn't run very fast. He didn't let the teasing bother him too much, because he knew that his parents and his sister loved him.

Mostly he played by himself. He made little boats and sailed them on the river. He watched frogs jump in the pond. He sat in the bushes and watched beavers build their houses in the stream. He went to the meadow and picked wildflowers for his mother, then he lay down and listened to the grasshoppers jump through the grass and watched the clouds make fantastic shapes in the sky.

One day some older kids came up to Shimon and demanded that he return the money he stole from Rebecca. Shimon didn't have any idea what they were talking about. He hadn't stolen any money. They said, "Nachum saw you take the wallet."

"I don't have Rebecca's wallet, and I never took it." The big kids moved forward to grab Shimon, but he jumped out of the way, ran around the corner, and mixed in with the crowd of people on the street. They called after him, "Shimon, return the money or you will be sorry."

The next day he came to school late so the big kids couldn't beat him up before school. After school he hid in a closet until they had left.

His parents asked him why he was so late in coming home, and he told them he was just playing. This went on for a few days. Then things got worse. Nachum and his friends spread the rumor that Shimon was a thief, so when Shimon passed other children, they would hold onto their book bags and mutter, "Watch out for the little thief."

The principal of the school called Shimon in and asked about the stolen wallet. "If you return it with the money, we'll just forget about it, but if we find you with it, you will be in big trouble." When Shimon said he didn't know anything about the money, his parents were called. "Look, we have a witness who says that he stole it," explained the principal.

Shimon said, "I don't have it—look in my book bag if you want." The principal opened it and there were only books.

The principal noticed a side pocket and asked, "What's in there?"

"Nothing. I never use it, but look if you want."

The principal opened it, and out fell a wallet.

"Then what is that?"

Shimon said, "I've never seen it before."

The principal looked in the wallet and, sure enough, it was Rebecca's.

Shimon's parents couldn't believe it. Their own son had stolen a wallet!

"But I didn't take it!" Shimon cried.

Rebecca said, "I had six kopeks in it and there is nothing in it now." She demanded that Shimon return her money.

Shimon didn't have six kopeks and didn't know how to get that much money. His father said, "I will pay the six kopeks, but you will have to repay me and you will be punished!"

Shimon told his friend, Sara, what had happened and she believed that he was innocent. Sara said, "Nachum is in my class, I have a plan." The next day Sara took a kopek, which she marked with a red dot and a black dot. She put the coin in her wallet and left it on a desk. She told Shimon to leave his book bag near by. Then they hid in the closet. They watched while Nachum took the money out of the wallet and then put the empty wallet into Shimon's book bag. After the recess, Nachum went up to the teacher and said that he saw Shimon take the money out of Sara's wallet.

Then Shimon and Sara stood up and told what they saw. Nachum was so surprised that he stood there stammering. Finally he blurted out, "They are the ones who are lying to protect Shimon."

Sara said, "Nachum, if you will show us the coin in your pocket, I will show you that the kopek has a red dot and a black dot on it. I put the dots there myself." Nachum showed them the kopek and, sure enough, it had red and black dots. Nachum finally had to admit taking it. He even admitted taking the money from Rebecca and putting the empty wallet into Shimon's book bag.

The principal held an assembly with all the students. He publicly apologized to Shimon and asked every student who had accused Shimon of theft to apologize as well. He told them that talebearing, falsely accusing someone of doing something wrong, or lying about others is very dangerous. "Everyone who has spread a rumor that Shimon is a thief must tell everyone to whom they told the rumor that it is false. That way everyone will know that the tale is not true. After they have done that, they must go to Shimon and say they are sorry."

Values

The principal's message to the students should be emphasized. Not only should people not steal, they should never spread or repeat tales about other people, especially if they do not know if they are true.

Questions to Discuss

Did anyone ever tell you something that another person did?
Did you know if it was true? Did you repeat it?

Suppose you know the story is true. Do you think it is okay to repeat it then? Suppose the story says something nice about someone.
Can you think of any reason why it still might not be a good idea to repeat it?

Why do you think the Torah tells us not to repeat tales about others?

Story-Telling Props and Tips

- wallet
- some money
- book bag

When Sara marks the coins, the storyteller may want to use large paper coins with red and black dots so that everyone can see them.

28

A CORNER FOR THE POOR

EMOR, Leviticus 21:1—24:23

In this Torah portion we learn about the festivals of the year. The Torah reminds us that when we harvest, we must share with the poor. This story tells how a man learned the importance of caring for those who are poor.

And when you reap the harvest of your land, you shall not reap all the way to the corners of your field, or gather the gleanings of your harvest; you shall leave them for the poor and the stranger: I am Adonai your God. (Leviticus 23:22)

"Oh no!" thought Simon, "there they are again! That whole family is always dressed in rags and looking for a handout. I'm glad that I cut the entire field already. Otherwise they would be swarming all over it like fleas on a dog, like flies on fruit, like bees after honey. If I'd left even a stalk of grain standing, they'd be all over it. Let them get jobs."

The family of poor and hungry people who approached the field looked tired. The children were barefoot. The father's face was gray. The mother was so weak that she had to lean on her husband. Simon walked out to the edge of his field to meet them.

"Move along," he called out. "There's nothing here for you. Don't be hanging around here."

The father approached him: "But sir, we are hungry. We haven't eaten in two days. We've just come to glean, to pick up the leftovers on the ground from the harvest."

"Move along," Simon bellowed. "Didn't I tell you there is nothing here for you?"

"Would there be a little something for the children? Even just a little water?"

"I told you to move along. I don't want lazy people like you hanging around here."

"I'd be glad to work for food. We all would."

"All the work's been done. Besides, I can't pay high wages. Do you think I'm made of money?"

All this time people in the neighboring fields were watching and listening to Simon. One of them called out to the family to come over to them for food.

Meanwhile a woman named Rachel went over to Simon and said, "Why did you cut your entire field? You know the Torah says to leave the corners for the poor."

"Mind your own business. It's my land. I can do what I want with it."

"But the land also comes from God," she said. "The Torah says that we should leave the corners of the field uncut, so the poor can take the grain. We are also supposed to leave the leftover sheaves of grain and fruits of the land for the poor."

"I told you," said Simon, "it's my land and I don't feel like helping those people. Let them work for a living."

"But it doesn't depend on how you feel. You owe it to the poor." Rachel reminded him, "You used God's land. You should give some of what you grow to the poor."

"They are just a bunch of fakers looking for a free ride," snarled Simon as he walked away.

That year there was a good harvest, but the following year there was very little rain in the mountains, and the river that ran though Simon's land was almost dry. Most of Simon's neighbors watered their land from wells that they dug, or from a nearby lake, but Simon had always depended on the river that ran right through his fields. He watched as the wheat dried up and died. He prayed for rain but no rain came. He watched his corn dry up and die. At harvest time there was nothing to harvest. He ran out of food and grew hungry. He still owed money for his land, and since there was no harvest at all, he lost his land. Simon became a wanderer, a beggar.

He went to his neighbors and asked to glean in their fields. They allowed him to take what he needed. Then he went to his neighbor Rachel and asked for work. Rachel told him she would give him a job during the harvest. Rachel was a fair boss. Simon worked hard and was well paid. At the end of the harvest, when Simon was ready to leave, he said, "You have been very kind to me. You let me glean and you gave me a job. You never mentioned that I didn't help the needy when I had my own farm with a good harvest. Thank you."

"I only did what the Torah requires," said Rachel. "I would never shame you by reminding you of what you had done in the past. You were a good worker too. I will loan you money to start another farm if you promise to help the poor."

Simon was so grateful that he was speechless. He did buy another farm, and he always shared the corners of the field with the poor.

Values

Even those things we may "own" really belong to God, since everything we have ultimately comes from the natural world that God created. We just use it for a while. In return for using what God has given us, we have to take care of the world and share its fruits with those who do not have enough. We also have to remember that when other people do wrong, we should not shame them.

Questions to Discuss

What things do you or your family own?
How do you think they might really belong to God?

What do you think you can do to take care of what
God has given you?

How can you share with the poor?

Story-Telling Props and Tips

• Garden tool
• Very simple hats for the poor family

Set up a basket and ask the children to bring in food for a food pantry and/or money to support groups that feed the poor.

29

MALKA DOESN'T WANT TO MOVE

BEHAR-BEHUKOTAI, Leviticus 25:1—27:34

Details of the jubilee year are a significant part of these two Torah portions. The jubilee was the fiftieth year, when land was returned to its original owners. This story tells about the difficulties a girl faces in moving back to her family's homestead, which she had never seen.

In this year of jubilee each of you shall return to his possession...Houses in villages that have no wall around them...shall be released in the jubilee.
(Leviticus 25:13,31)

Malka was tired and hungry. Her feet were sore from walking all day, but she was happy. She was going back to her home, where all her friends were. Early that morning she pretended that she was going to school, but instead she ran away from the new home where her family had moved to just a week ago.

Now she would be able to play in the woods near her old house, and sit and listen to the water gurgle in the stream. There were trees to climb—great trees, which had branches in just the right places for climbing. There were places she could go in the early evening and sit very quietly, watching the deer munch on the sweet grass. Her friends could come too.

She sat down to rest for a few moments and thought back to the day her parents told her that they were going to move.

"Why?" she had asked.

"Remember all the stories grandpa told you about where he grew up?" they said.

"Yes."

"Didn't that sound like a wonderful place?"

"Yes."

"Well we are going to move there."

Malka's grandfather had told her about the farm where he grew up: how there were cows and horses, and how he used to ride his horse over the hills to visit his friends, and how they would take food and blankets and ride into the mountains to go camping. It sounded very exciting then, but Malka liked where she was living. She had her friends and plenty of places to play. Of course, the idea of riding a horse did sound exciting.

She remembered asking, "Can I get a horse like grandpa had?"

"Well, I don't think so," her father had replied. "There are no horses there now. There are houses where the fields used to be. But we will have a nice garden, and there are fields outside the village."

Malka was downhearted. "Then why are we moving?"

"Because that is where your great, great, grandfather settled. This is the jubilee year. The people who lived there since then have it only until now. Grandpa couldn't keep it because he was so poor. He had to sell it, but the Bible says that land goes back to the original owners after fifty years. This is the jubilee and we are going back."

She remembered her parents saying, "It is a much nicer house than the one we have now and we will be closer to the town. You know how much you like to go to the town market with us."

"But what about my friends?"

"Oh, you will see some of them on market days when they come to town. You'll have fun. When we move, you'll be able to go to the village any time you want. And besides, the school is a better school."

Malka remembered how she had told her parents, "I don't care about that school. The school here is fine and I don't care about the town. I want to stay here."

"Well, you can come back and visit your friends, but we are going to move after next fall."

Malka got up from her rest, took a drink from a stream, and walked on. She had only another two hours before it would get dark, and she was anxious to get to her old home before then.

As she walked, Malka thought of all the fun she had had the summer before, playing with her friends. She remembered counting the days until she had to leave. Each day was a day closer to the dreaded move. Her parents were packing things to take and throwing out things they didn't need anymore. Malka prayed that God would prevent the move. Just before school started, wagons were loaded with everything the family owned. Her friends stood sadly beside the wagons and waved good-bye. They called out, "See you soon in town!" "Come back and visit!" They meant well, but Malka knew that even though they might meet once in a while and they might even visit, it would never be the same.

Malka stopped to rest again. She took out her last piece of bread and ate it, hoping it would give her the energy to walk faster.

She remembered that it was just a week ago that she took the long ride in the wagon to their new house. She had to admit that it was beautiful. There were all kinds of flowers in the garden. A dozen children crowded around to look at her and her family as they unpacked the wagon. She felt as though they were looking her over. She even heard one of them say that she looked like a dumb country kid.

A few days later her parents took her to her new school. Her teacher seemed nice enough, but at lunch the other students ignored her, except the few who eyed her from a distance. She looked at her clothes—they were different from the clothes the kids in this town wore. She felt out of place and she ate alone. A few of the older girls came and told her to move, saying that she was sitting in their place. She was miserable and wanted to go back home. Right then and there she decided to run away and go back to her real home. Maybe she could live with the people who now lived there. If not, one of her friends was sure to take her in.

A half hour later she could see her old house from the distance and she broke into a trot. No one was there. The new family probably hadn't arrived, she figured, so it would be all right to stay there. She climbed in through a window and looked around. Without all their things and without the rest of her family, it didn't seem the same. She looked to see if she could find something to eat, but there wasn't anything there. She decided to go over to her friend Shimi's house. They always had lots of good things to eat. Shimi's mother would certainly let her stay.

Shimi and his family were surprised to see her! They invited her in and asked her to eat with them.

"How come you are here?" Shimi's mother asked. "Did your family change its mind?"

"No. I came back myself. I don't like it there."

"Do they know you came back here?"

"Well, I left a note that I didn't like my new school and my new house."

"You mean they don't know where you are?"

Malka shrugged.

"Your parents must be frantic," said Shimi's mother. "Finish eating. We'll hitch up the wagon and bring you back."

Malka was very sad. She tried not to cry.

Her parents were angry with her but very glad to see her. Her father said, "I know you didn't want to move. It's hard to leave your friends, and the school where you know the others, and they know you, but give it a chance. You will like your new home. And you will make new friends. Remember, this land has been in our family for many, many years—since long before your grandfather. It has been in our family since Moses brought our people to this land."

When she went to school the next day, a tall, thin boy came over and asked her questions about where she came from and what kinds of games she played there. The boy told her about some of the games they played. Then he asked, "How do you like living here?"

"I wish I were back with my old friends," she said.

The boy said, "Give it some time. I moved here last year. No one paid any attention to me for a long time. It's not like in the country, but you will get to know the other kids and it will work out." Then he invited Malka to meet him and his friends after school.

After a few weeks Malka felt at home. And on market days she introduced her old friends to her new friends.

Values

There are many reasons for a family to move. Malka's family moved because it was the jubilee year and her family was able to move back to their family home. Today people move because of work, or because they want to live in a different house or neighborhood. Moving to a new home and neighborhood, leaving old friends, and entering a new school can be very difficult for children as well as adults. It is important for everyone to welcome newcomers and to make them feel at home.

Questions to Discuss

Have you ever moved to a new home? How did you feel?
....

Do you know other children who have moved into your neighborhood or are new to your school? How to do think you can make
them feel more welcome?
....

Story-Telling Props and Tips

- walking stick
- canteen for water
- bread

30

PLACES OF HONOR

BEMIDBAR, Numbers 1:1—4:20

In this opening portion of the Book of Numbers the tribes are each assigned a place where they are to camp around the Tabernacle, with the eastern side being the most honored. This story tells why the tribes of Judah, Issachar, and Zebulun were chosen to encamp on that side.

The Israelites shall camp under the banners of their... house. Camped on the front, or east side...Judah... Issachar...Zebulun. (Numbers 2:2,3,5,7)

When the tribes traveled in the desert, they camped around the Tabernacle, where the Israelites worshiped God. At that time the Tabernacle was a special tent that was made of beautiful red, blue, and purple cloth. Imagine how striking this bright and colorful tent must have looked in the desert, with drab sand, rocks, and little tufts of plants all around. The priestly families put their flags closest to the Tabernacle and camped there because they were the ones who performed all the ceremonies. They also had to pack up the Tabernacle when the Israelites traveled and set it up again when they stopped to camp.

All the other tribes camped farther back, behind the priestly families. It was considered an honor to camp on the eastern side, because that is where the holiest place in the Tabernacle is located. That is the direction from which the sun rises, the sign that God has created a new day.

Obviously all the tribes couldn't be on the east, because some tribes had to protect the Tabernacle from the other sides. So the problem was which tribes should be on the east. How would they decide?

They each wanted the honor:

Reuven said, "I am the firstborn of Jacob and my tribe should be on the east. The oldest son deserves to be honored in that way."

Moses answered, "Being the oldest son or the firstborn is no reason to be in a place of honor. Isaac, Jacob, and Joseph were all the honored ones but they were not the oldest."

Simeon said, "I am powerful. My tribe will fight for the people. No one can defeat us in battle."

Moses said, "Power is not the most important thing to us. We may need to protect ourselves, but that is not why we are a people. The Tabernacle stands for peace, not war."

Asher said, "My tribe should be on the east because we are the richest tribe. We will bring trade, we will find work for people, and we will make our people rich."

Moses said, "We all need to have enough money to live, but riches are not what are most important."

Each of the other tribes came forward except for Judah, Zebulun, and Issachar, who were leaders of their own tribes. They were more humble. Moses asked them if they wanted to give a reason why they should be on the east. They didn't really think they were any better than any of the other tribes, so they didn't say anything.

Moses asked each of them, "Are you sure? Each of you has something special to contribute to your people. The tribe of Judah will be praised because you will serve all of Israel. The tribe of Issachar will love the land and settle it peacefully, and Zebulun will live on the shore of the sea and welcome visitors from other lands.

Judah spoke up: "Everything you say is true, but each of the tribes has something special to contribute. None of us is more important than the others." The leaders of Issachar and Zebulun nodded in agreement.

When Moses heard that, he announced that these three tribes would be on the east, because they were humble and didn't think they were better than any of the others. That is how those three tribes— Judah, Issachar, and Zebulun—were chosen to camp on the east side, the place of honor.

Values

The choice of Judah, Issachar, and Zebulun points out what we should value most—service to others, peacefulness, good relationships with others, and being kind to strangers. Those tribes didn't think they were entitled to a special honor or position over the other tribes. In the story Moses pointed out that being the oldest son, or the most powerful, or the richest doesn't make someone the most important person. A humble person does not value himself or herself less because they also value others. Judah, Issachar, and Zebulun didn't say they were less important than the others were—they each understood that they were an important part of the people of Israel. They simply said that they were not more important than the others were.

Questions to Discuss

What is special about your friend or brother or sister?

What is special about you?

Does this mean that you or they are more important than others?

Story-Telling Props and Tips

- flags with the names of the various tribes
- a sword for Simeon
- gold pieces for Asher

31

BETH'S BLESSING

NASO, Leviticus 4:21—7:89

These chapters of Leviticus include the "Priestly Blessing." It is this blessing that Jewish parents customarily recite over their children at the beginning of the Sabbath. This story, set in modern times, shows how this is a blessing that is unconditional.

May God bless you and keep you; May God show you favor and be gracious to you; May God show you kindness and grant you peace. (Numbers 6:24-26)

Beth and Laura loved to play baseball. They would take turns pitching and batting. While Beth loved baseball, she hated doing chores. One afternoon after school Beth was supposed to clean out the birdcage, make her bed, and water the plants in the house. Instead she went out to play baseball. Laura pitched her an easy ball and Beth connected solidly—too solidly. The ball sailed across the street and right through the Yeagers' window. Both girls ran and hid behind Beth's house. The Yeagers didn't seem to be home, because no one came to the window to see what had happened and no one came outside to find whoever had broken the window.

When Beth's mother came home, she asked Beth what she had been doing.

"Nothing. Just my homework," said Beth. It was a lie. A little later Beth's mother called her: "Beth, I see you didn't do any of your chores."

"Oh Mom, I guess I forgot. Like I said, I was doing homework."

"Okay. Do them now, please. Remember, you asked for extra things you could do for extra allowance money so you can go to the amusement park. You have to do the chores if you expect to be paid. And you shouldn't need reminding."

Beth rolled her eyes.

After dinner Mr. Yeager came over.

"I believe this ball belongs to Beth. It has her name written on it."

Her mother thanked him. "Where did you find it?" she asked.

"In my living room."

"How did it get in your living room?"

"I think it came through the window."

"Uh oh," her mother said. "I'll take care of this. Tell us how much the window cost, and we'll pay for it. I'm very sorry. I didn't know. Beth never said anything."

She went up to Beth's room. "Beth, how did your ball get into the Yeagers' living room?" she asked.

"Yeagers' living room? I don't know," answered Beth.

"Beth," said her mother, "Mr. Yeager came over and gave me a ball with your name on it. His window is broken. There is a connection, isn't there?"

Beth finally admitted she had been playing with Laura and hit the ball through Mr. Yeager's window. "It was an accident," she said. "We played for only a short time. I needed a break from my homework."

"Let's see your homework," asked her mother.

Beth looked at the floor.

"Well?" her mother insisted.

"Actually, I didn't do any homework. We went out to play, I broke the window, and then you came home and I did the chores."

Beth's mother sat down, "Beth you are in real trouble. First of all, you are going to pay for the window. We'll pay Mr. Yeager, but you will pay us. You'll do the chores, and we'll use that money for the window. You won't go to the amusement park and you are grounded for a week. The worst part of this is not that you broke a window. That can happen. But you denied it, you lied about it, and you didn't take responsibility for what you did. You should have left a note for Mr. Yeager telling him that you had broken the window and would pay for it. That's what you should have done. But worse than that," her mother's voice got higher and louder, "you lied. You lied about the homework, you lied about the chores, and you lied about the window. That is inexcusable. I'm very angry about this. Now go to your room and do your homework. No TV either. And while you're at it, I want you to write Mr. Yeager a note telling him that you are sorry you broke the window and that you will pay for it."

The next day was Shabbat. Beth came to the dinner table. They lit the candles to welcome Shabbat, and then her parents each placed a hand on her head and said the blessing for her which they said every Friday night: "May God bless you and keep you; May God show you favor and be gracious to you; May God show you kindness and grant you peace." That was the blessing the priests said in the Bible. She always felt special and loved when they did that. After they said the blessing, they gave her a kiss and told her, "We love you."

After dinner she asked her mother, "How come you gave me the blessing this week, since I'm grounded for doing lots of bad stuff?"

Her mother said, "Some things have to be earned, like money to go to an amusement park, but our love and our blessing for you belong to you no matter what. They belong to you whether you do well in school or not, whether or not you practice the piano; even if you misbehave, you always have our love and our blessing. It is because we love you that we get so disappointed when you do the wrong things, and it is because we love you that we try to teach you the right way to behave." She smiled and gave Beth a kiss: "Shabbat Shalom."

Values

It is important to tell the truth and to admit when we do something wrong. Then we can repair any hurt or damage we caused. It is also important for parents to love and say the blessing for their children, even if those children misbehave.

Questions to Discuss

Did you ever damage something or lose something that belonged to someone else? What did you do? Did you find a way to repair the damage or replace whatever you lost?

Do you think your parents love you even if you misbehave and they are angry with you? Why?

Story-Telling Props and Tips

- a baseball and glove
- baseball hat
- a notebook and school books
- Shabbat candles

32

CARRYING THE FLAG

BEHA'ALOTCHA, Numbers 8:1—12:16

These passages from the Torah describe how each tribe would follow the person holding that tribe's flag when the people of Israel were traveling in the desert. This story tells how the flag carrier of the tribe of Judah was chosen.

And the flag of the...children of Judah went forward.
(Numbers 10:14)

Soon after the Israelites left Egypt, the Egyptians chased after them. The Israelites were at the edge of the Sea of Reeds when they saw the Egyptians coming, and they were terrified. Moses then raised his staff and urged the people to start walking into the water. The very first person to step forward was Nahshon, the great leader of the tribe of Judah.

As the leader of the tribe of Judah, Nahshon had the task of choosing the person who would have the honor of carrying the flag of the tribe as they wandered through the desert. There were many worthy people who wanted the honor. There were people from important families who wanted Nahshon to choose them, and there were others who promised him wealth if he would choose them. Some people even threatened him.

Nahshon decided that there was only one way for him to be fair in coming to a decision. The people who wanted to carry the flag would tell him why they thought they were worthy of this honor. He decided to sit behind a screen so he could hear them but couldn't see them. In that way he wouldn't know who the people were and he could never be accused of playing favorites.

Starting early in the morning, people lined up outside his tent, and one by one they came in to speak to Nahshon. Every person was called up by a letter of the Hebrew alphabet so Nahshon wouldn't need to use their real names.

"Alef" said that he was a great warrior. On the way out of Egypt, he took swords and spears they could use to fight. He said that the desert was dangerous and it was important to have a brave fighter at the front of the tribe to rally the people if there was a war.

"Bet" said that he was a great hunter. He told Nahshon that food would be the major problem for the people. He would not only carry the flag, but he would teach the people to hunt with spears, traps, and arrows.

"Gimmel" said that he was a great runner. Gimmel felt that it was very important for all the tribes to be in touch with one another. He could be a messenger and go back and forth between the tribes.

"Dalet" said that he had a very loud voice. It would be important to be able to speak in a very loud voice to all the people when they were gathered together, so they all would hear. When he called out loudly to show Nahshon how loud he could make his voice, Nahshon had to hold his ears.

Nahshon listened to all the rest of them, from Hay to Tav, but he didn't find the right person. All of these people could do very important things, but Nahshon wanted someone who had the most important qualities of the tribe of Judah. He wanted a person who would be an example for others to look up to.

The next day he was walking through the camp and found himself in the area where young orphans were cared for. These were children whose parents had died and who had no one else to look after them. Most of the time they looked very sad. However, this time he heard the sound of music being played and children laughing. He stopped to listen. Someone was playing a flute. Then the music stopped. He heard a soft voice speaking to the children with kindness. He peeked around a corner and he saw a young woman who was not much older than the children. As she spoke, the children listened closely and smiled. She obviously loved them and they loved her. Nahshon sat down to listen. She told the children that even though they had no parents, she and the people of the tribe loved them and they would always be taken care of. In addition, they should know that even they can do important things for their people. The children asked how. She told them that they would enter the Promised Land when they got older, and the hope of the whole people rested on them.

Nahshon waited until she finished, went over to the young woman, and said, "You are kind and wise. We would be honored if you would carry the flag of our tribe."

And that is how it came to be that Shira bat Tzuriel v'Hanah (Shira, the daughter of Tzuriel and Hanah) came to carry the flag of the tribe of Judah.

Values

We too face the task of caring for the weakest and most vulnerable among us. We should look for leaders whose kindness and wisdom will lead them to care for the needy and who will be devoted to caring for our children, because our children are our future.

Questions to Discuss

How would you have tried to find the right person without just choosing someone because he or she was your friend or because someone important told you to choose that person? What qualities would you look for? What kind of person would you want?

Story-Telling Props and Tips

• a flag with the lion of Judah on it, placed on a pole
• a sword, a bow and arrow
• a pair of sneakers
• a megaphone
• signs with the Hebrew letters *alef, bet, gimmel, dalet*

Also ask a child who can play the hallil (recorder or flute) to play when Shira plays in the story.

As you tell the story, hold the flag until the end, when the child who plays the instrument gets to hold it. You might give him or her the flag to keep.

33

CALEB HAS A MIND OF HIS OWN

SHELAH LECHA, Numbers 13:1—15:41

While the Israelites were traveling in the desert, God told Moses to send out some people to explore the land of Canaan— the Promised Land. Moses chose one person from each tribe. Caleb was the representative from the tribe of Judah. After the twelve scouts returned from Canaan, only Caleb and Joshua reported that the Israelites would be able to conquer the land. This story tells about the kind of person Caleb was and why he was so different from the others.

Send men to scout the land of Canaan...
Of the tribe of Judah, Caleb... (Numbers 13:2,6)

From the time that Caleb was a young boy, he would do the right thing even when other children were misbehaving. If all the other children were going to do something that he thought was wrong, he was able to decide what was right for him to do and he wouldn't go along with them. When he grew up, he continued to be known as someone who could think for himself and make up his own mind.

Caleb was also very brave. One time he heard that a little girl was lost in the desert. Caleb took some water and food and set out to find her. He stayed out in the wilderness all night until he found her huddled near a cave. Then he put the little girl on his shoulders and carried her all the way back to the camp.

While the Israelites were wandering in the desert, he was chosen from the tribe of Judah to be one of twelve people to go into the Promised Land, to see what the land was like and then to tell the other tribes what they had seen. He was chosen because he could make up his own mind and because he was brave.

The twelve scouts traveled through small villages, speaking with the people, tasting the food, and noting where there were wells with clean, fresh water. It was a wonderful land, as if it were flowing with milk and honey. There were grapes so big that one cluster had to be carried on a pole between two people. However, even though the land was very rich, some of its people were so unfriendly that they wouldn't even give them water. Almost all the other scouts were afraid.

In some towns the men seemed very big. Most of them were seven feet tall with very big muscles. They also wore armor and carried knives, swords, and spears. They were very fierce. Every day one of the other scouts, named Igal, would tell Caleb, "We cannot take over the land. These people will never let us."

But Caleb told him that everything looked fine. The other scouts immediately said, "Are you crazy? The people who live in this country are powerful, and the cities are very large and well protected. Their warriors are the size of giants and will eat us alive. We will look like grasshoppers to them. Leave us out of this."

Caleb told them that the land was good and that they would be able to overcome any difficulties in overtaking the land.

"But what about the fierce warriors?" challenged Gadi, another scout.

"There are very few of them," said Caleb. "And look at them. They wear so much armor, they can hardly move. If any of them get rough with us, we can certainly take care of them."

"You are dreaming," said another spy, Ammiel. "We could never defeat them."

Just then one of the local warriors approached them and snorted, "What are you snooping around here for?" Caleb told him that they were just traveling through, but the warrior drew his sword and got ready to swing at them. Caleb moved back, took out his slingshot, put in a round stone, and whirled it around. The warrior let out a fierce cry and charged at him with his sword. Caleb let go of the stone and hit the warrior in the shoulder, calling out, "The next one goes to your head. Just back off and leave us alone." The warrior grabbed his shoulder and howled in pain. Caleb and the other spies walked on.

"Okay," said another scout, Sethur, "we were lucky that guy was an oaf and you made a lucky shot."

Caleb knew that he couldn't do anything to change their mind, so he just kept to himself.

When they returned to Moses, only Joshua and Caleb understood how good the land really was and how well they could live there. They were the only two who were brave enough to see that they could actually live in the land that God had promised to them. They were the only ones who could think for themselves.

Values

Caleb was brave and had the ability to think for himself. When he went into the land, he made his own decisions about what his people would be able to do there. He made his own decisions, even though nearly everyone around him had a different opinion. Caleb understood that God had promised the Israelites a good land, and Caleb was able to see beyond all the problems, to a land that could be a wonderful place for them to live.

We too may see a world with many problems: poor people, war, illness, and a damaged environment. Some people may say that many of these problems cannot be solved, but, like Caleb, we also should understand that God has given us a good land, a world full of wonder, and we should see how good it really could be.

Questions to Discuss

How do you think Caleb felt when all the other scouts disagreed with him?

How do you think the other tribal leaders felt about Caleb? Do you think they thought Caleb was brave or do you think they thought he was foolish?

Can you think of a time when everyone said that something could not be done but you or someone else was sure that it could be done?

Story-Telling Props and Tips

• sword
• slingshot
• large paper cluster of grapes carried on a pole

34

THINKING FOR HIMSELF

KORAH, Numbers 16:1—18:32

During the years when Israel was wandering in the wilderness, there were times when the people were very unhappy. At one such time a man named Korah tried to lead a rebellion against Moses. At the beginning of the story of the rebellion, a person named On (pronounced like "own"), the son of Pelet, is part of Korah's group. By the end of the story On is no longer mentioned. This story explains why On dropped out of Korah's group.

Now Korah...with Dothan and Abiram...and On...took men...and they rose up against Moses. (Numbers 16:1,2)

When On, the son of Pelet, was a child, he wanted others to like him. In that way he was no different from other children. The problem was that he wanted them to like him so much that he allowed them to take advantage of him. Some of the boys would tell him they needed him for a game and then, when better players came along, they kicked him off the team. He didn't object, because he was afraid they wouldn't like him. If they knew that someone had just made some cookies, they would convince him to steal them by telling him that they were allowed to have them. Of course On was the one who got caught and the other boys pretended to be just passing by. In school some of the girls would claim they needed his help with homework, but they really wanted him to do it for them.

It would seem that people could convince him of anything. They also played jokes on him. One of the older children told him, "Quick, go to Benjamin's house and tell him I need some shore line." Then Benjamin would send him to Shimon and Shimon to Reuven and on and on until someone was kind enough to tell him they were playing a joke on him, because shore line wasn't a special kind of rope but rather the edge of the water along the beach. Meanwhile the others had a big laugh. Still, On didn't complain.

When he went to buy things, people would tell him that certain nuts had miraculous powers, that a certain kind of bread had a magic potion in it, or that a pot had a magic genie in it.

There was nothing wrong with his brain. He just believed people. Since he was always honest, On couldn't believe that anyone else would lie or cheat or play tricks on him. He knew that some of the things people told him didn't make much sense, but he wanted them to like him and he was afraid to complain to them.

One day On was called over by Korah: "We want you to be in on something very important. We think that Moses and Aaron have too much power here. Everybody is equal. Why should we all have to listen to them?"

"What are you planning to do?" asked On.

Korah said, "We are just going to the Tabernacle, and we will offer incense there. That will show that everyone can do it. We will always be remembered as the people who freed the people from Moses and Aaron ruling over them. Don't you want always to be remembered in that way?"

"Well . . . ," answered On, "I'm not very sure of the whole idea."

"Of course you are. I knew you were a good fellow."

On began to object: "But . . . "

Korah interrupted: "No ifs, ands, or buts about it. We'll be famous because we are doing something very, very important. Don't you want to be important?" demanded Korah.

"Yes . . . "

"Of course you do. Don't you want to be famous?"

"Well . . . "

"Of course you do." And with that Korah told On to meet them the next day. For now Korah was busy. He was going to a meeting with the others.

"Can I go too?" asked On.

"No, of course not," said Korah. "Look, if you want to be part of us, you have to listen and take orders. Do you understand that?"

"Yes . . . "

"Of course you do. Now listen carefully. You are to be here at daybreak tomorrow. And don't be late or you'll be in real trouble."

On, the son of Pelet, was bothered by all of this. If they were trying to stop Moses and Aaron from being so bossy, how come Korah was being bossy with him? He sat down to think. His friend Elisheva came by.

"On, you look worried," said Elisheva.

On told Elisheva what had happened. Elisheva didn't tell him what she thought he should do. She just said, "You are a smart fellow and you will figure out what is the right thing to do."

On thought some more. He was more confident that he could make the right decision. The more he thought, the less he liked Korah, but he showed up the next day to see what would happen.

What happened that morning shocked him. Korah spoke to Moses very rudely. Moses was so upset that these people would attack him that he literally covered his face and, with tears coming down his face, prayed to God.

Later in the day Korah came to On and told him, "Wasn't that great this morning. We really showed Moses a thing or two. We are going to win this."

On, the son of Pelet, told him, "I don't want any part of what you are doing. You were rude to Moses. You hurt him deeply. You are doing a terrible thing. Leave me out of your plan."

Korah muttered, "Good riddance. Who needs you."

It's a good thing that On left Korah's group because he could see that Korah and the others were trying to rule over everyone else. They complained about Moses being bossy, but they were acting the same way.

On, the son of Pelet, learned that he really could think for himself.

Values

We all want people to like us, but first we all have to like ourselves, respect ourselves, and think for ourselves. On, the son of Pelet, had a difficult time at first, but when his friend Elisheva encouraged him to think for himself and showed confidence that he could make his own decisions, then On really did begin to think for himself and he dropped out of Korah's group.

Questions to Discuss

Have you ever been fooled or taken advantage of?
Have people ever played a trick on you?

Have others ever tried to get you involved in
something that you realized was not a good thing?
How did you deal with these situations?

Story-Telling Props and Tips

- a ball
- a plate of cookies
- a homework notebook
- a few nuts
- loaf or piece of bread
- a pot

35

THE DONKEY'S TALE

HUKKAT-BALAK, Numbers 19:1—25:9

The story of Balaam and his donkey is one of the great stories of the Bible. Balak, the king of Moab, was afraid of the Israelites, so he sent messengers to Balaam, a seer or prophet, telling him to put a curse on the Israelites. At first Balaam refused. Finally God told Balaam to go with the messengers but to say only what God told him to say. Balaam saddled his donkey and went with them. In the end he blessed, rather than cursed Israel. "The Donkey's Tale" retells the story from the point of view of the donkey, and it shows how people can bring blessing on others.

Balaam saddled his ass and departed with the Moabite dignitaries. But God was incensed at his going; so an angel of Adonai placed himself in his way as an adversary. (Numbers 22:21-22)

First off, I wish you humans would get the words right. I'm a donkey. An ass is a wild animal that lives out in the fields. I'm civilized. I work with people and in towns. You call that a domestic animal. And when an ass is a domestic animal, we are called donkeys, thank you.

Second, you should understand that I can speak. Donkeys speak. All animals speak—to each other, to other animals, and even to humans. But humans, who think they are so much smarter than us, need long strings of words, like these, to say anything. We, on the other hand, can say everything with a few simple sounds.

Now Balaam and I have a deal. He can ride on my back and I'll take him where he wants to go. In return, he feeds me and cleans out my stall. It's a pretty good deal for me. I'm strong and I like to go places anyway. There is one other thing about Balaam. He believes in God. None of the other people in our area believe in God, but he does. I like to work for him because he speaks to God a lot and I listen in. The problem with him is that he doesn't always do what God tells him to do.

One day Balak, the king of Moab, sent messengers to Balaam, and they told him that the king wanted him to curse Israel. Balaam should have known without asking that he couldn't do that, but he asked God anyway. And what do you think? God told him he shouldn't do it. Balaam sent the messengers away. They came back again. This time they promised to make him a rich man. When he heard about the money, lots of money, his ears perked up and he said, "Well, stay over tonight. Maybe God will have something else to say." By morning he had made himself believe that God had told him he could go with them. Humans are so good at fooling themselves, especially when it comes to money. And they think they are smarter than animals! Did you ever know an animal that would go against God for money?

Now I had a problem. Balaam got me all ready to go on a trip that I knew God didn't want him to take. I didn't know what to do. I had a deal with him. I had made a promise to take him wherever he wanted to go. Yet I never thought he would want to do something that God didn't want him to do.

Fortunately, God sent a messenger with a sword who stood in the middle of the road. I thought Balaam saw the messenger, but he kept telling me to go forward. At the last minute I saved both of us by going off into the field next to the road. Still he didn't understand and he kept beating me to get back on the road. By this time the birds saw what was going on and they called, chirped, and squawked something fierce. They created such a racket that you would think Balaam would have realized that something unusual was happening. And humans have the expression "Bird brain!"

Then the messenger stood at the spot on the road where there is a wall on both sides. Again Balaam kept going. I was afraid he would drive us right into the sword, so I pushed up against the wall and squeezed Balaam's foot. Balaam still didn't get the picture and he beat me some more. This time the cows in the field on the other side of the road saw what was happening, and they were lowing and bellowing. Still Balaam didn't have a clue. And humans think cows are stupid!

The road became so narrow that there was no way to get around the messenger, so I just lay down on it. Balaam beat me some more, but there was no way I was going to try to get around God's messenger. Finally I got good and angry and I had to use all those human words: "Why are you hitting me? Don't you see the messenger of God blocking your way? Don't you understand that God doesn't want you to curse Israel no matter how much money Balak offers?" Only then did Balaam see the messenger. All the animals had seen the messenger and understood what God wanted, but Balaam never saw what the rest of us saw until it was almost too late.

The messenger told Balaam that he could go to Balak, but he should say only what God told him to say. Balaam finally got the picture. I took Balaam to the first mountaintop and, instead of cursing Israel, Balaam blessed Israel. Balak was furious. I took Balaam to the second mountaintop. Again Balaam blessed Israel. Balak was furious and told Balaam not to say anything further, but Balaam told Balak he would have to do whatever God told him to do. So Balak said to try a third mountaintop, because he hoped that God would finally let Balaam curse Israel. I took Balaam to the third mountaintop. The people of Israel were encamped in the valley below. The beautiful ark was in the middle with all the colorful tents around it. Balaam said the words that the people of Israel still say in their morning prayers: "*Ma Tovu Obalecba Ya'akov, Mishk'notecba Yisrael*—How goodly are your tents O Jacob, your dwellings O Israel."

It was a proud moment for me. Balaam finally learned what all the animals already knew: God rules the world and we should do what God wants us to do. True, Balaam took a long time to understand that. He needed all those words, while the animals understood and could do with only a few sounds for everything. But after all, he is only a human being and you have to make allowances.

Values

Even people who believe in God sometimes have a hard time understanding what God wants of us. Often they are tempted to do the wrong thing because of money or the promise of being famous. But like Balaam, if we listen and want to learn, we can be a blessing to those around us.

Questions to Discuss

Do you have any animals? Do you think they ever "speak" to you?
....
Are you ever tempted to do the wrong thing?
....
How do you learn what is the right thing to do?
....

Story-Telling Props and Tips

- gold coins
- birds, cows—either pictures or toy models
- tents—either a drawing or a piece of fabric or paper in the shape of a tent

36

JOSHUA HELPS HIS PEOPLE

PINHAS, Numbers 25:10—30:1

Moses was very old and would soon die, so God brought Moses to a high mountain so that he could see the Promised Land of Israel in the distance. Moses, realizing that he would not live much longer, asked God to appoint a new leader. Then God chose Joshua to take Moses' place as leader of the people. This story tells about Joshua's special qualities, which led God to choose him.

Adonai said to Moses, take Joshua, the son of Nun, a man in whom there is the spirit...and set him before...the entire community (Numbers 27:18-19)

Moses was such a great leader that God would have a very hard time finding the right person to lead the people after Moses' death. Didn't Moses do great things? Hadn't he led the people out of Egypt? Hadn't he gone up on Mount Sinai to receive the Torah? Hadn't he protected the people in the wilderness? Now Moses was about to die and God had to choose someone else.

One day as the people of Israel were traveling in the desert, a woman ran up to Joshua yelling that the Amalekites had just attacked the Israelites in the back of the line. That is where all the old, the sick, and the small children were, since they couldn't walk as fast as the others. Amalek had surrounded them, so Joshua had to do something very fast.

Joshua immediately called his soldiers. Then he called on the men and women who were doctors, storytellers, singers, and good listeners. Next he called on children and old people who he knew were kind-hearted.

Joshua's lieutenant complained, "What are we going to do with all these people? They will only get in the way. We will end up having to rescue them from Amalak, and they will slow us down on the way." Joshua said only that he should be patient and he would see how important they would be.

Joshua and his crew marched all night past the camps of their people, gathering more and more help as they went. At daybreak, just as the purple and red dawn appeared, they looked over the hill at Amalek's camp that surrounded the weakest among the people of Israel. Amalek had many soldiers and they had good weapons. Some of Joshua's men did not think they could defeat the soldiers of Amalek. Joshua pointed off to the side and showed them the tattered camp of the Israelites, which Amalek had attacked. He told them they had no choice and that they must protect their people. Joshua then divided his soldiers into three groups. He told one group to move behind the rocks on one side and the other group to move to the other side. The third group would go right down the middle.

He told the doctors, storytellers, singers, and others who would help the weak and injured Israelites, to be ready. Then Joshua blew the first call on the shofar, the *tekiah* (one long note), to signal his soldiers to attack the army of Amalek from three sides. Amalek and his men were surrounded and had only one way out, so they ran into the desert.

Then Joshua blew the shofar a second time. This time it was a *shevarim* (three shorter notes). This was the signal for the doctors, storytellers, singers, and good listeners to go into the camp of the Israelites. They gave water to the thirsty, bandaged wounds, and comforted the old people. They gathered the children and sang songs with them. There were many who were very afraid, so the good listeners went to comfort them.

Finally Joshua blew the shofar a third time, the *teruah* (nine very short notes), and brought everyone together. He said, "We can never again allow our children, our old people, and our sick to fall to the back of our people so they are without protection. They are part of us and we must take care of them."

That is why Joshua was chosen to lead after Moses. Not only was he a great warrior, he also cared about his people.

Values

What Joshua taught and did in his time holds true for our time as well. We still need to protect our people when they are in danger of being attacked. We still need to make sure that the children, the elderly, and the sick are cared for. We cannot leave them behind.

Questions to Discuss

Why did Joshua bring doctors, storytellers, singers, and good listeners with him when he went to rescue his people?

How do you think the good listeners helped?

What do you think we can do today to help children, old people, and those who are sick?

Story-Telling Props and Tips

• a book for a storyteller
• song for the singer
• bandages for the doctor
• shofar (an actual shofar, which can be blown, or a cardboard replica of one)

37

SHIRAH LEARNS ABOUT SHARING

MATTOT-MASEI, Numbers 30:2—36:13

After the people of Israel left Egypt, they faced many hardships. Mostly they worried about having enough food and water. In this story some people made foolish promises to God hoping that this would encourage God to provide water. This story tells how Shirah and the other Israelites learned about the importance of sharing the little food and water that they had, and also about not making foolish promises to God.

If a man makes a vow to Adonai...he shall not break his pledge. (Numbers 30:3)

The Israelites set out from Rameses...and came to Elim...and encamped at Rephidim; it was there that the people had no water to drink. (Numbers 33:5,9,14)

Shirah, who was only 11, lay on her straw mattress and listened while her parents talked about escaping from Egyptian slavery.

"It will be wonderful to leave Egypt, to be free," said her father in his deep voice.

"Yes," said her mother, "but how will we survive in the desert?"

"I have faith in God and in Moses," replied her father. "We will find a way to get water and food."

"I have faith in God too," said her mother, "but I still worry about it."

Shirah was excited about leaving, but she too was worried. Would there really be enough to eat and drink? Would she be able to walk all day, day after day, in the hot desert? How would they protect themselves from wild animals?

Two days later the word came for them to leave. Everything was done in a hurry. They grabbed what they could from the little shack they called home, put it all on their backs, and started out. Shirah was small and had to walk twice as fast as the grown-ups just to keep up. It was hard walking in the desert and it was hot.

After everyone had a chance to rest from the adventure of crossing the sea and the quick escape from Egypt, Moses led them next to a place called Elim. There they found 12 springs of water and 70 palm trees. Each of the tribes camped by one of the springs. They had wonderful fresh water to drink and the palm trees provided delicious dates to eat. Shirah felt as though she were on a picnic. They stayed there for a whole week to rest. Moses told them, "Right now you have plenty of food because you need to rest and gain strength for the long journey, but you must learn not to waste and you must learn to share." Before they headed for Rephidim, they picked all the dates they could reach and collected all the water they could carry.

When they arrived in Rephidim, all they found was a dried-up well and a few scraggly trees without dates. Some of the people wondered if Moses knew what he was doing. Some argued over the few dates that were left. Others complained to Moses, "Why did you bring us here?"

Moses told them, "You will always have just enough but never anything extra. In order for all of us to survive, we will have to share. If anyone takes too much, then someone else will not have enough. God is teaching you to depend upon one another, to help one another, and to share with one another."

But some people claimed that they were entitled to more than the others. One man said, "I am a descendent of Joseph, who was Jacob's favorite son; I should have more." Another said, "I can lead everyone to the next place to camp; I should have more." Still another, who carried a sword, said, "I can defend the people from attack; I should have more." So these people took more and therefore some of the others didn't have enough.

Moses was very angry. "There is no way for us to get more food and water. We have to care for one another." Then he made them divide up the food. Shirah took a jug of water over to an old man who couldn't carry much water himself, and she gave some food to a woman with a small child.

The following week was very, very hard: they ran out of water. Everyone was terrified that they would soon die of thirst. Shirah's mother looked very worried. She prayed, "Dear God, if You lead us to water, we will spend our lives serving You." Many others made vows promising God they would do anything as long as they could find water. Moses told them that it was not necessary to make vows to find water. The people argued, "We have to do something."

"Okay," he said, "if you feel that you have to make a vow to God, think very carefully about what you promise."

Some people were too frightened to pay any attention to Moses. One woman vowed that she would eat only bread and water for the rest of her life if only she could have water. It was a terrible vow. Who could live on only bread and water? Her family brought her to Moses: "She will get sick if that is all she eats. Can't something be done to cancel the vow?" Moses thought about it and agreed that a vow this dangerous should be canceled.

The people were panicking because there was no sign of water. They walked though the wilderness of Zin, a rocky, desolate place with not a tree in sight. There was not even a green patch of ground. Nothing. No sign of water. Only the tan and red rock, and the sandy ground. People grumbled against Moses. People grumbled against God. People were angry with one another. Some people were just silent and weak from walking without having had water to drink or enough food to eat.

At night they camped at the edge of a valley and everyone fell asleep, exhausted. But Shirah lay awake looking up at the stars and listening to the night sounds. She thought she heard water. She listened carefully. Was she imagining it? She listened again. Yes, it sounded like water running, like a small waterfall. She woke up her parents and told them. They listened too and they heard it. They ran to Moses and told him. He did not look surprised. "Yes," he said, "it is water. As soon as it is light we shall go down into the valley. There is a waterfall there and a small pond. But remember, we all have to share."

They found water and food there, just as Moses said they would. As they continued on their journey, they always found just what they needed. From then on, they shared what they had and there was enough for everyone.

Values

We are all on a journey in a world in which God has provided enough for all of us, but we still have to remember to share what we have with people who don't have enough. That means that we have to help the poor. Two ways that we can do this is by donating food to food banks or teaching people a trade so they can get a job.

Questions to Discuss

Are there any times when you have shared your own things with other people?
....

What might you share with the poor?
....

What is a famine? What can we do to help people during a famine?
....

Story-Telling Props and Tips

• dates
• jug of water

38

ASHER THE JUDGE

DEVARIM, Deuteronomy 1:1—3:22

The Torah teaches us that judges must be fair and honest. This story tells about a good judge who was fair and honest even though others tried to get him to take their side and to be dishonest.

You shall not be partial in judgment. Fear no person, for judgment is God's. (Deuteronomy 1:17)

A long time ago there was an honest and learned Jew named Asher, who lived in a small town. Because of his honesty and wisdom, the people of the town asked him to be a judge.

When people had a disagreement they would come to Asher. Each person would tell his or her side of the story, and after checking all the important books of law and wisdom, Asher would decide who was right. The people respected him and accepted his decisions.

One day a very good friend of Asher, named Shimona, came to him with her neighbor. The neighbor said that Shimona's bull had gotten loose and trampled all her strawberries. Shimona said that the bull had been tied up—it wasn't her fault that the bull got loose. The neighbor said, "But you didn't tie up the bull with strong enough rope. You should pay me for all the strawberries he ruined."

Asher decided that the neighbor was right. Shimona should have made sure that the bull didn't damage anyone's property, and he told Shimona to pay for the strawberries.

Shimona was outraged. How could Asher go against her? She threatened never to speak to Asher again if he didn't change his decision. Asher told her that he had to do what was right; he had made a decision based on the law. Then he reminded Shimona, "You are being unfair to expect me to do something dishonest because we are friends."

Another time two people came before him. One was a man who sold fruits and vegetables at the market. The other said that she bought a basket of apples and that the fruit on the bottom was rotten. The shop owner said that all the apples were fine when he sold them.

Asher spoke to some people who saw the woman empty the basket when she got home. They said that the apples on top of the basket were good but the ones at the bottom were rotten. Asher decided that the customer had been cheated. The shop owner had to give the customer good apples and pay a fine for pretending that all the apples were good.

The shop owner threatened Asher saying, "You are a terrible judge and I will make sure you are removed from your position; I will see that no one in this town will ever speak to you again."

A few days later Asher noticed that people in the synagogue walked away from him and wouldn't speak to him. Then he was visited by a group of the leaders of the town who told him that the owner had accused him of asking for a bribe. They said that he would have to step down as judge.

When Asher told them that the charge was false, the town elders reminded Asher that the shop owner was very important in town because he gave many people work and donated money to the poor. The elders were afraid that the store owner would leave town if the decision was not changed. Asher told them that if they allowed this one man to bend justice to suit himself, the man would be able to do anything he wanted to do.

Since no one would listen to him and the people in town would not speak to him, Asher decided to pack up his things and move to a new town. It was very sad for Asher, because he loved the town. As he was packing, Shimona came to visit. She said, "I saw how honest you were. You wouldn't side even with me when you thought I was wrong. I was angry with you, but you were right to do what you did. Now I want to make sure everyone understands how honest you are."

"How are you going to do that?" asked Asher.

"Tell me who was in the court the day the shop owner came in. They can tell the elders that you didn't ask for a bribe and that the shop owner threatened you."

Asher told her who the other people were and Shimona went to visit them. Some were afraid to speak out, but several were very angry about the way the shop owner had spoken to Asher and how he had threatened Asher.

After Shimona spoke to the town elders, they set up a special court. The elders listened to the people Shimona brought and they listened to the shop owner. They asked him if it was really true that Asher had tried to bribe him. Finally the shop owner admitted that he had lied. He said that he was angry with Asher for deciding against him, but now he was very sorry. He admitted that he had cheated the woman and said that he would pay her. He also agreed to tell everyone that he had not told the truth about Asher. He said, "Asher is a fair and honest judge."

Values

Most of us are not going to be judges, but we are sometimes asked to side with people just because they are friends or because they are rich or powerful. A real friend will not ask us to do something dishonest.

Questions to Discuss

Did a friend ever want you to side with him or her, even if you thought the friend was wrong?

Did a friend ever want you to lie or to do something dishonest because he or she was your friend? What did you do?

Why do you think the farmer had to tell everyone that he hadn't told the truth about Asher and that Asher was really an honest judge?

Story-Telling Props and Tips

- strawberries
- apples
- gavel

39

THE MOST BEAUTIFUL HORSE

VA'ETHANAN, Deuteronomy 3:23—7:11

The last of the Ten Commandments tells us not to covet. That means that while we might want some of the things other people have, we cannot try to take those things from them. This story tells about two young women and a beautiful horse and what can happen when people don't obey the commandment not to covet.

You shall not covet...anything that is your neighbor's.
(Deuteronomy 5:18)

Long ago there were two young women, Ruth and Miriam, who lived on farms next to one another. They were both the same age; they both had long, dark hair and brown eyes; they both did well at school. The only problem was that Miriam always thought that whatever Ruth had was better than what she had. She thought that Ruth had nicer hair and nicer eyes. She wanted to be as smart as Ruth, even though they did equally well in school. Most of all, Miriam wanted Ruth's beautiful horse, Sus. [Pronounced *soos*, Sus means horse in Hebrew.]

Sus was a gorgeous deep brown stallion with a white patch on his nose. When he had just been brushed and stood in the sunlight, his coat shimmered. And when Ruth rode him through the fields, his long tail trailed out behind him like a beautiful banner. Miriam would go out to the edge of the field between their farms and stand behind a tree to watch Ruth ride Sus. Oh how she would love to have Sus! It was the most beautiful horse she or anyone in her village had ever seen. If only she had Sus, then people would come out to watch her ride. Then when she rode into the village, everyone would turn around and admire her. She thought and thought about how she could get Sus for herself, but she could not figure out how to get him.

She offered to buy him from Ruth but Ruth said that she would never sell Sus, no matter how much money anyone offered her. "Sus," she said, "is like a member of my family. Besides," Ruth added, "you have a very beautiful horse too. Why would you want Sus?"

Miriam replied, "Because my horse is not quite like Sus. No horse is like Sus."

Miriam finally had an idea. She wanted Sus so badly that she wrote up a fake paper which said that because her father had done a favor for Ruth's father, Ruth's father would give Sus to Miriam when she was 13 years old. Then she signed the names of both fathers. Since both fathers had died years before, Miriam was sure no one would know what she had done.

Then she went to Ruth and said, "I was going through some old papers and I found this agreement. Since I am now 13 years old, you must give Sus to me."

Ruth was shocked. She couldn't believe that Miriam would lie about such a thing, and yet she couldn't believe that the story was true. Something must be wrong, but what could it be? Her father's signature looked okay, so with tears running down her face, she led Miriam to the barn and gave Sus to Miriam. Sus looked confused. He didn't understand where he was being taken. He didn't like being ridden by strangers either. When Miriam tried to ride him, he bucked and shook his head. She kicked him with her heels and hit him with her whip. Ruth pleaded with Miriam not to hurt Sus. Miriam finally got him under control and rode off.

Of course Ruth was very sad. She took the paper into the house and sat staring at it. She took out some of her father's old papers and looked at the signature again. Sure enough, it looked like his signature.

The next day she went to visit her aunt, who lived in the next town. When she told Aunt Zipporah about the horse, her aunt said, "That paper is a lie. I remember giving Sus to your father. He had an extra plow and I had an extra horse. So we just traded. In fact I still have the plow with your father's initials, which he carved into the handle. I think that your father did many favors for Miriam's father and not the other way around. Show me the paper Miriam gave to you, because it must be a fake."

The next day Ruth came back to her aunt's house and showed her the paper. Aunt Zipporah said, "It is a fake, and I'll tell you why. This signature says Avram Yitzchak ben Shlomo. Your father didn't sign his name that way until after another man named Avram ben Shlomo moved into the area. Before that, when this paper is supposed to have been signed, your father signed only Avram ben Shlomo.

Then Aunt Zipporah and Ruth went to the rabbi and told him the story. They called Miriam. When Aunt Zipporah told her side of the story, Miriam finally admitted that she wrote the paper herself to get the horse.

The rabbi looked at Miriam and said, "You broke three commandments. You lied about the paper, you stole the horse, and you coveted your neighbor's horse. 'Coveted' means that you wanted what someone else had and you were even willing to cheat that someone to get it. You will have to return the horse, pay a fine, and promise never to do anything like that again. You also must learn to be satisfied with what you have."

Values

Sometimes we may want something that someone else has. We may think it is better than what we have, and we may imagine how wonderful it would be if we only had what that person has. We should first try to be satisfied with what we have, but if we want something we think is better, we must always buy it honestly and never try to cheat anyone to get it.

Questions to Discuss

Have you ever wanted something belonging to someone else?

Do you agree with the rabbi's punishment for Miriam?

Story-Telling Props and Tips

- riding hat for Ruth and for Miriam
- piece of paper representing the "agreement"
- picture of a beautiful horse or a toy horse

CHAIM THE JEWELER

EKEV, Deuteronomy 7:12—11:25

Soon the Israelites will enter the Promised Land, where they will prosper, and where they will have plenty to eat and drink. Moses reminds the people that they cannot forget to thank God. This story, about a boy who is helped by a woman, shows that what we have comes not only from our own efforts, but from what God has given us and from what others have taught us.

When...your gold and silver have increased, and everything you have has prospered, beware lest...you forget Adonai...and you say to yourselves, "My own power... [has] won this wealth for me." Remember it is your God who gives you the power to get wealth.
(Deuteronomy 8:12,13,14,17,18)

Once there was a famous jewelry store in Warsaw, Poland, called Ravinovich's. There are a lot of jewelry stores around the world that might be famous among rich people, but Ravinovich's was also famous among the poor people of the neighborhood. Why, you might ask, would poor people be interested in a jewelry store? Don't they have to worry about getting enough food to eat, paying the rent, and buying coal for the winter without thinking about jewels? That is true, but each week the poor went to Ravinovich's. In fact their best "customers" were poor. Let's begin our story with a poor boy named Chaim.

When Chaim was a small boy, he lived in a narrow and dirty alleyway near Krochmalna Street on the other side of Warsaw. His father worked very hard delivering coal, which was used for heating in those days. When Chaim's father came home from work, his face and hands would be black from coal dust. Since the family could not live only on what his father made, his mother helped to take care of other people's children. They managed to have just enough money, but nothing extra.

Chaim had a lot of time to explore other parts of the city. One day when he was on the other side of Warsaw, he noticed a sign in a jewelry shop: "Person needed to clean shop." Chaim went in. He figured he could help his family if he could earn even a little money. The jeweler, Mrs. Ravinovich, looked him over and disappeared to the back of the store to make tea. Chaim waited for her. He looked at some jewels that she had left on the counter. He had never seen anything so bright and sparkly in his life. He loved the way the light went through them. He noticed the rings of gold and silver in the showcase. Chaim got tired of waiting. He was about to leave when Mrs. Ravinovich came out from the back. She looked at the jewels, looked at Chaim, and said, "You're hired." Then Chaim knew that it had been a test to make sure he was honest. He later found out the "jewels" were just glass.

Mrs. Ravinovich told Chaim to sweep the floor, wash the showcases and the windows, and polish the big brass doorknob.

Mrs. Ravinovich thought Chaim was a good worker and let him watch while she drew designs for jewelry. Chaim also loved watching her shape gold and silver, along with diamonds, rubies, emeralds, and pearls into beautiful pins, earrings, and bracelets.

Soon Mrs. Ravinovich was showing Chaim how to make jewelry too, and in time, she hired Chaim as a jeweler. Chaim worked hard each day. He even closed the shop, except for Friday afternoons, when Mrs. Ravinovich told him that she would close the shop.

Years passed and Chaim's designs and beautiful work became known throughout Warsaw. Soon wealthy people from all over the city were coming to admire his jewelry. Mrs. Ravinovich sent him to Paris, London, and New York to look at the latest designs, to sell his jewelry, and to buy the best that those cities had to offer. In time, Chaim's work became more sought after than Mrs. Ravinovich's, but she didn't mind at all. She was proud that her student had surpassed her in skill. She was as proud of Chaim as if he were her own son.

Mrs. Ravinovich was getting old. Her fingers would no longer make jewelry, so she waited on customers. Soon she found it hard to stand so long. She told Chaim that she would retire and that Chaim could have the shop as his own. Chaim did not know what to say. How could he just accept a gift like that? Mrs. Ravinovich had paid him well.

"Chaim," Mrs. Ravinovich explained, "this shop didn't come out of thin air. When I was young, a jeweler taught me how to make jewelry. Other people had enough faith in me to lend me the money to open the shop. My customers trusted me to be honest with them and they were honest with me. So you see, I didn't do this all by myself. And you helped me too. I can't repay all of the people who helped me, but I can do for you what they did for me."

Mrs. Ravinovich then asked Chaim a question: "Did you ever wonder why I sent you home early on Fridays and closed the shop myself?"

Chaim told her that he never thought much about it. He just figured that since Chaim had to go across town to his family, he had been given extra time to get ready for Shabbat.

Then Mrs. Ravinovich told him, "I have always had one very strict rule, and you can have the shop only on the condition that you follow this rule. Every week I set aside money for the poor." She told Chaim that he must always help people if they asked. She said that every Friday afternoon the poor of the neighborhood would come to her shop and would be given money. Many of them count on that help. It was well known among the poor that they could always get help at Ravinovich's. She told Chaim that he would have to promise always to continue doing that. Of course he agreed.

Chaim was surprised, because he had seen some other shopkeepers chase beggars away. He knew that his father gave to the poor, and he did too, out of his pay. But it never occurred to him that a shop owner would set aside money from his or her earnings every week.

Mrs. Ravinovich explained, "Do you think I earned this on my own?" Chaim looked around. He didn't see anyone else in the store making jewelry.

"Chaim," Mrs. Ravinovich went on, "these jewels are God's creation. This gold and silver are God's creation. All I do is shape it and polish it. Look at my hands—look at my eyes. I couldn't do even the shaping and polishing without them. I owe everything to God and I have to give back some of what was given to me. And," she added, "I have enough faith in you that you will run the shop wisely and honestly and that you will help someone the way people helped me and I helped you."

So that is how Ravinovich's jewelry store became famous among the poor and how it continued to be famous among the poor after Chaim took it over.

Values

It was one thing for Mrs. Ravinovich to feel obligated to share with the poor, but she also felt the responsibility to help a young man learn a trade, just as she had been taught. Whatever we have, we have because God provided us with what we needed and because others helped us learn the skills we need to make our way in the world. That is why we need to help others.

Questions to Discuss

Why did Mrs. Ravinovich feel it was her obligation to give money to the poor?

The Hebrew term for what Mrs. Ravinovich did is tzedakah, which means "righteousness" or "justice." Why do think what Mrs. Ravinovich did would be called tzedakah.

What do you think God has given you? How do you think you can "pay back" God or show your appreciation to God and others for what they have given you?

What things have others taught you?

Story-Telling Props and Tips

• bag of "coal"
• jewels of all kinds
• a tzedakah (alms) box
• a broom for Chaim

41

THE WISE KING AND THE VISITOR

RE'EH, Deuteronomy 11:26—16:17

This Torah portion tells about Pesaḥ (Passover), Shavuot (Feast of Weeks), and Sukkot (Tabernacles), which are the three major festivals when Jews would go to the Temple in Jerusalem for the celebration. The only festival about which the Torah says that you will "have nothing but joy" or be "altogether joyful" is Sukkot. What is so especially joyful about Sukkot? How should we express that joy? How should we observe the holiday so that it will be especially joyful? More generally, what is the proper way to celebrate any important time in our lives? This story touches on these questions.

"...you shall hold the Feast of Booths for seven days. You shall rejoice in your festival...you shall have nothing but joy. (Deuteronomy 16:13,14,15)

Once upon a time there was a Jewish king who was known far and wide for his wisdom. People from every corner of the world would come to see him and try to learn from him. He and the people in his kingdom knew all about science, mathematics, and medicine.

A great queen, who had vast riches and loved to show off her wealth by throwing big parties, heard about this king and sent him a letter: "We have heard that you have some very unusual holidays and ways of celebrating them. Since we have great celebrations in our country, we want to come and learn new ways from you."

The king wrote back and invited her to visit him.

The queen traveled over mountains with snow-covered peaks and across broad green valleys in order to visit the king during Passover.

When she arrived, she saw that he was happy to celebrate Passover, but he was also very serious. She could see that he spent a great deal of time in deep thought. He walked in his garden, his hands clasped behind him, thinking his wise thoughts. She asked him, "Why are you so serious? Since this is the celebration of how God brought the Jewish people out of slavery, you should be happy. You should have a giant celebration."

He replied, "I am happy, and we do have a special celebration—the Passover seder—with songs, stories, and wonderful things to eat. But Passover is also a serious time. We have to think about the Exodus from Egypt. We have to think about what God did for us, and we have to think of how best to use our freedom."

The queen went home disappointed, but when she heard that the king was having another celebration seven weeks later, she again traveled over mountains with snow-covered peaks and across broad green valleys to visit him on Shavuot. Again he walked in the garden deep in thought. He sat on a bench and looked at the pond covered with lily pads, he listened to the frogs croaking, and he watched the birds flitting from tree to tree.

Again the queen saw what he was doing and asked, "Why are you so serious? Isn't this a happy time? Isn't receiving the commandments at Mount Sinai a good enough reason to be happy and celebrate?"

The king said that he was very happy. "And," he added, "the commandments, which show us how to live good lives, are reason for us to be happy. But it is a serious time as well, because we have to think about what Torah and the commandments mean to us in our time. We do celebrate, but we also study, and think about the commandments."

Again the queen went home disappointed.

Months went by. Rosh Hashanah and Yom Kippur came and went, and then it was time for Sukkot. Since she heard that Sukkot was especially joyful, she decided to return to the king once more. Again she traveled over mountains with snow-covered peaks and across broad, green valleys.

This time when she arrived, the king was sitting in his sukkah. It had four thin walls, which he had decorated. Instead of having a regular roof, the top was covered with bamboo poles, which allowed a few rays of sunshine to creep through and make shadow designs on the walls. The king sat sharing wine, delicious food and pieces of fruit with his family and friends. They sang songs and said special prayers to God. In between they all danced joyously.

The queen saw all of this and remarked, "Sukkot is a joyous holiday and you seem to be enjoying yourself, but sitting in this funny little hut doesn't seem like much of a celebration."

The king asked, "What do you think would be the proper way to celebrate?"

"Well," she answered, "you have a palace. Why don't you throw a grand party? You could invite all the important people in your kingdom. You could buy something special that you and your family wants. You could do something that would spread your fame even further. For example, you could have a special statue made of yourself."

The king listened carefully and then said, "On Sukkot we can be completely joyful, since the entire festival is devoted to thanking God for the harvest. But we have better ways to celebrate than what you suggest. We spend time in a simple sukkah, rather than in the grand ballroom of the palace, in order to remind us how much we depend upon God. Otherwise we might not really be able to thank God properly. We don't need to buy anything special, because God has given us the gifts of this earth that God has created—there are no better or more important gifts. And the idea of this festival is not to make me famous, but to thank God."

The king went on: "Big parties, buying things, and wanting to be famous do not bring nearly as much joy as the complete joy of Sukkot."

When she heard what the king said, the queen and all her servants bowed low to show how much respect they had for the king's wisdom.

Values

When the Jewish people have something very important to celebrate, it is done simply and joyfully. It is not a matter of how fancy the celebration is, or a matter of buying presents or of trying to be famous, but of thanking God and rejoicing. Sukkot is the festival when there is nothing but joy, because on Sukkot, we simply thank God for what we have.

When we celebrate any important time in our lives, at least part of that celebration should be devoted to thanking God for the goodness that has come to us.

Questions to Discuss

Why do you think the queen was disappointed?

What special times do you celebrate? How do you celebrate them?

What does this story tell us about how we should celebrate special occasions?

Story-Telling Props and Tips

- crowns for the king and queen
- a symbol for Passover such as a piece of matzah
- a symbol for Shavuot such as a Torah scroll or picture of the tablets of the Ten Commandments
- a symbol for Sukkot such as a picture of a sukkah or a lulav

42

THE GOOD QUEEN

SHOFTIM, Deuteronomy 16:18—21:9

Among the most important aspects of this Torah portion are the rules that the kings of Israel must obey. This story about two queens, Berachah and Ezedek, shows what can happen when these rules are not followed.

...you shall be free to set a king over yourself...he shall not keep many horses...nor amass silver and gold to excess...he shall have a copy of this Teaching [the Torah] written for him on a scroll. (Deuteronomy 17:15,16,17,18)

Long ago, in a faraway country, there was a good queen named Berachah, which means "blessing." She was given that name because she was a great blessing to her country. Berachah followed the Torah and was very careful not to take all the gold and silver in the country for herself. Also she did not have many horses for fighting wars because her country had no real enemies. Most important, she always kept a copy of the Torah near her to study it and to be guided by it.

One day Queen Berachah set out on a voyage to visit other kings and queens so that there would continue to be peace between all the nations in her area. She brought wise people with her who would learn new ideas from the other nations.

The journey was a very long one and, after being away for almost a year, she decided it was time to return home. As her ship was passing some dangerous rocks, there was a fierce storm. The captain tried his best to save the ship, but it sank and only a few people survived.

Fortunately the queen was among them. She, two other women, and a man climbed up onto a large piece of wood and, after drifting for two days, they washed up on the shore of an island. They were very tired, hungry, and thirsty, so they immediately started to look for food and water, which they found near the beach. Unfortunately, there were no other people on the island and there was no way to get off the island and back to their home.

Meanwhile the people in her country heard that she had been on her way home and that her ship sank. They assumed that she had died. They were very sad and decided that the only thing they could do was to crown a new queen. After much discussion they chose Berachah's cousin, whose name was Tzedek, which means justice.

After Tzedek was crowned queen, she told the people that a neighboring country would soon attack them and that she had to have an army of thousands of soldiers on horseback to protect the nation. She taxed her people and soon had a big army. Then she kept taxing them more and more and with the money bought more and more jewels and gold for herself. The people grumbled, but since she had a big army to protect her, there was nothing the people could do. Soon they no longer called her Tzedek, or justice, but instead they began to call her Etzedek, unjust or wicked. Also the neighboring countries saw that Queen Etzedek was building a big army and thought that she was getting ready to attack them, so they also built big armies and decided that instead of waiting for her to attack them, they would attack Etzedek's country first.

In the meantime, Queen Berachah and the people with her were found. A ship was passing near the island, and the crew saw the queen waving from the shore. They picked her up and were soon on the way to return her to her kingdom. When Queen Berachah arrived back in her country, she hardly recognized it. There were soldiers everywhere. The people who had been happy and smiling when she left now looked sad and worried. She decided to dress in ordinary clothes so no one would recognize her. Then she heard talk of war. She was told that the generals from her country were leading the army toward the neighboring border and that the neighboring army was ready to attack.

Quickly she went to the border and stood up on a hill, wearing her crown and long royal coat. She told the generals from her country that she was back home and that they should stop right there. The generals were so surprised and happy to see her, as were all the soldiers, that they immediately gathered around her and brought her back to the palace. The neighboring generals heard that there was no longer a danger of war and they went home as well.

When Queen Berachah arrived at the palace, she told Queen

Etzedek that she had violated all the rules of being a queen. For that reason Etzedek could no longer remain queen. The last thing the generals did before they disbanded the army was to lead Etzedek out of the palace. Then they established a seven-day holiday to celebrate the homecoming of their beloved Queen Berachah.

Values

All leaders, whether kings, queens, presidents, principals, or captains of a team, must lead fairly and honestly. They must not take advantage of their people.

Questions to Discuss

Do you know anyone who has ever been the president of a club or the captain of a team? Did they have rules they had to follow?

What would usually happen if a leader didn't follow the rules?

Why does the Torah give these rules?

Story-Telling Props and Tips

- a crown for both Berachah and Etzedek
- something to represent a horse, such as a hobbyhorse, or even a picture of a horse
- a sword and/or spear
- a paddle, oar, or something to suggest the ship
- a ship captain's hat

43

REMEMBERING AMALEK

KI TETZEI, Deuteronomy 21:10—25:19

When the Israelites were wandering in the wilderness, they faced many dangers. One of those dangers was being attacked by hostile nations such as the people of Amalek. At the end of this section of the Torah, it says that we should remember what Amalek did to the Israelites in the desert. This story is about why we remember both the good and the bad things that happen to us.

Remember what Amalek did to you on your journey, after you left Egypt...when you were famished and weary and [he] cut down all the stragglers in your rear.
(Deuteronomy 25:17,18)

One evening, after Israel had left Egypt and had been wandering for many years, an old woman sat with a group of children by a campfire in the desert. The dancing flames warmed them in the chill of the desert night. The stars shone in the huge dome of sky. She said, "I have told you about the Exodus many times, but tonight I am going to tell you parts of the story that you have never heard before."

The children loved to hear some of the old stories over and over again, but tonight they were doubly excited to hear a new addition to the story. They all edged a little closer and leaned forward because they didn't want to miss a word.

"The Exodus was a wonderful time," she began, "although many of us were frightened. On the night we left Egypt, we had to leave so quickly that we had to take the unbaked bread dough with us. We literally threw the few things we owned into baskets, which we carried or loaded on donkeys, tied the goats and sheep together, and left in a panic. We were afraid that Pharaoh would change his mind and not let us go. Well, at first Pharaoh was so afraid of God that he did let us go, but then he changed his mind and chased after us. By that time we had arrived at the sea. We were terrified because we had no place to go. Pharaoh and his soldiers were behind us and the sea was in front of us. Even if the way were clear in front of us, there was no way we could move very fast. There were thousands of people, including children, and also many animals. Some of us thought we were done for."

"Now, I wasn't in the front, but I heard that as soon as God told the people to move forward, a fellow named Nahshon, the son of Amminadab, walked into the sea. Everyone was amazed that Nahshon walked across. It was very shallow there, and the tide was out, so we could follow him and walk across on the thin ribbon of land. By the time we were across, Pharaoh caught up to us, but he couldn't drive his chariots after us. The ground was so soft that they just sank into the mud."

"Were we relieved! That night there was a giant celebration. Miriam led all the women in dancing and song. Some women played tambourines. We spent the entire night dancing and singing and celebrating and thanking God for freeing us from Egypt."

The old woman looked at the shining faces of the children reflected in the light of the campfire. She hesitated but she knew she had to tell them the whole story, not just about the times that were good, the times when they escaped danger.

She took a deep breath and said, "But it wasn't all good. There were many hard times too."

"I must now tell you about one of the very bad times. We were making our way through the wilderness, which wasn't easy to begin with. It was very hot. There was little water and very little food. We found just enough to stay alive."

The old woman paused, looked up at the vast black sky spread with stars that glittered like diamonds, and took another deep breath. Then she said in a whisper, "To make matters worse, we were attacked. We were attacked by Amalek."

She paused a moment and added, "We were prepared to defend ourselves if we had to, but we purposely avoided getting into fights with anyone. Our guards were leading us through a pass when Amalek attacked us from the rear. It was terrible. The people who were weak or old or sick usually stayed near the rear because they couldn't travel as fast as the others. Amalek attacked and killed innocent people who were old and weak and sick. Everyone was in mourning, whether they were related to the victims or not. It took us a long time to get over the loss of those people. In a way we still haven't, because the Bible says, 'Remember what Amalek did to you.'"

She looked at the children. They looked sad, and the old woman felt bad about telling them such a sad story, so she explained, "I am telling you about this because the Bible wants us to remember both the Exodus from Egypt and the attack by Amalek. The bad times as well as good times are part of our story. We certainly don't want to forget the people Amalek killed. And we mourned so deeply for them that we just can't ignore what happened. After all, we remember people in our family who died, don't we, even if remembering brings back some of the sadness. That is why the Bible tells us to 'Remember what Amalek did to us.'"

The old woman looked out at the sky, way in the distance, as if she could see into the future. Then she turned to the children and said, "There may be times again when others may attack our people, but we will always survive. We will always live to celebrate the good times and to praise God, who made heaven and earth."

Values

The Jewish people have experienced both joy and sadness, just as we have in our own lives. We remember both kinds of experiences, because both are part of us.

Questions to Discuss

Personal memories

What are some of your best memories?

Do you have any memories of sad times?

Do you have any memories of someone who has died?
(Here, be cautious and especially sensitive. A relative or friend of one of the children may have died recently. The goal is to have them experience the importance of memory to us and not bring back a lot

of pain. Yet, in cases where a child may have faced the death of a loved one, this exercise may be a helpful way to deal with that experience.)

Why is it important to remember both happy and sad times?

Memories of the Jewish people

Show the children a gragger. On what holiday do we use a gragger? What do we do with a gragger? Why do we make noise? Whose name do we blot out?

Tell the children that the story we just told was about Amalek, who was the great, great, great, great grandfather of Haman. Amalek also attacked our people. Every year just before Purim we remember what Haman's ancestor did to us.

On Passover we recall our suffering as slaves in Egypt and we remember how God freed us. On Yom Hashoah, Holocaust Memorial Day, we remember the terrible suffering of our people in Europe; but on Yom Ha-atzmaut we celebrate the founding of the State of Israel. Why is it important to remember both the sad and happy times in our people's history?

Story-Telling Props and Tips

• basket with clothes
• staff of Moses
• tambourine, drum, recorder
• hat and sword for an Amalakite soldier

44

YAFFA'S WAGON

KI TAVO, Deuteronomy 26:1—29:8

This portion in Deuteronomy teaches us to give a tenth of what we have to the poor. This story tells about the adventure of a farmer who followed that teaching.

When you have set aside in full the tenth part of your yield...and given it to the...stranger, the fatherless, and the widow...you shall declare...I have obeyed Adonai my God. (Deuteronomy 26:12,13,14)

Yaffa was a farmer. She planted cabbage, peppers, and tomatoes. She raised chickens that laid eggs, and she had a few cows for the milk.

She read in the Torah that she should set aside a tithe, or one tenth of her crops, to support the community and the poor. She thought about the Torah and she thought about all that she grew and raised on her farm. She worked hard, but she knew that it was God who created the earth. It was God who taught the seeds how to come up. It was God who created the chickens so that they laid eggs, and the cows so that they gave milk. Yaffa was very thankful, and to show her thanks she decided that after she sold her eggs, milk, and vegetables, she would set aside one tenth of everything and give it to the poor.

If there were 10 cans of milk, she put aside one can; for every 20 dozen eggs out, she put aside 2 dozen; and for every 100 pounds of tomatoes, she put aside 10 pounds. Every few weeks Yaffa would put all this food in a wagon. In the evening, she would pack ice around the milk to keep it cold, and then go to bed so that she would be well rested for her journey the next day to visit the poor children in a nearby town.

On one such morning, when Yaffa came out of her house, she was shocked that the wagon was gone. She looked behind her house. She looked around the side of the barn. It wasn't there. She couldn't imagine where it went. Finally it dawned on her that someone must have taken it. Not only was the wagon missing but her horse, Sally, was missing too.

Quickly she saddled up her other horse, Brimstone, and went out to look for the wagon. She followed the wagon tracks to the main road, but soon the tracks looked like the wagon tracks from other wagons and she couldn't follow them.

Meanwhile the person who stole the wagon decided to take all of the eggs, milk, and vegetables to the market and sell them for a good price. Sally trotted along at a good pace but wondered why a strange person was driving the wagon. The thief was already thinking of all the things he could buy with the money. But when they came to a fork in the road, Sally wouldn't take the road that went to the marketplace. She loved the children in the nearby town and looked forward to the apple they always gave her. Besides the person driving the wagon didn't speak to her nicely the way Yaffa did, and Sally didn't like that. The thief called to the horse, cracked the whip, stopped, got out, and tried to lead her into the town where the market was, but the horse wouldn't budge. Sally insisted on going in the other direction. And there was no sign to say where that might be. The thief decided that there wasn't much choice but to go where the horse wanted to go.

After a while, the thief came to another crossroad, and one of the signs pointed to the market town, but the horse just kept going on its own way. Finally, after a long journey, Sally stopped in front of a large house. There were many children there. A man came out and said, "Ah, I see Yaffa sent you with the food for the children. Is she all right?"

The thief muttered, "Yes Yaffa is fine." The children helped unload the wagon. Then, after the children fed Sally an apple, she turned around and started trotting back home. The thief had to run to catch up and jump on. His only hope now was that maybe he could sell the horse and wagon or at least take them home. But the horse headed straight back to Yaffa's house. There was nothing the thief could do to make the horse go right or left. The thief hoped that he could find someone to buy the horse and wagon before he got back to Yaffa's house.

Meanwhile, Yaffa was out looking for Sally and the wagon. She knew that if Sally got out of the barn, she would probably head straight to the children. There were days when Yaffa just climbed into the back of the wagon and went to sleep because Sally knew the way. Yaffa rode Brimstone out and she soon came upon the thief driving the empty wagon. Of course the thief didn't know who Yaffa was, so Yaffa turned around and got in front of the wagon. She called to Sally, gave Brimstone a gentle nudge, and off they all went. Sally was practically flying. The thief, who didn't know what had happened, was desperately trying to hold on. Sally galloped, pulling the wagon at a frightful speed until they found the town sheriff. The thief was so terrified from the ride that he just sat frozen on the wagon seat and the sheriff easily arrested him.

So in the end the children got their food and the thief was caught.

Values

Everything we have comes from God and the world that God created. The Torah wants us to take care of the earth and to make sure that people everywhere have enough to live. Yaffa understood that idea, so she set aside some of what she had for the poor.

Questions to Discuss

Why do you think the Torah teaches us to share with the poor?

What kinds of things could you share?

Story-Telling Props and Tips

• basket of vegetables
• eggs
• milk bottle
• toy horse or hobbyhorse
• sheriff's badge

Moses Waits for Everyone

NITZAVIM-VAYELECH, Deuteronomy 29:9— 30:20

As we near the end of the Book of Deuteronomy, Moses gathers all the people together to speak about the covenant with God. This story tells about how a little girl thought she had missed the gathering.

You are all gathered before Adonai: your heads, your tribes, your elders, and your officers, even all the men of Israel, your little ones, your wives.
(Deuteronomy 29:9-10)

When Rina heard that Moses had called all the people together she was very excited. She loved to see him with his long white beard and his staff.

On the morning of the big day, as Rina was getting ready, her friend Rebecca came running over. "Come quick," Rebecca said, "there's a new baby lamb, a female; she's the cutest little thing I ever saw." Rina told her mother she would be right back and ran to look in the sheep pen. Sure enough, there it was, just a little ball of wool. The lamb's mother was licking her. "What shall we name her?" asked Rebecca. As they were thinking of names, Rina noticed that Melech, a large ram, had blood on his fur, and they went to take a closer look. Poor Melech was lying on his side whimpering. He had big cuts on his face and neck and he had lost a great deal of blood. It looked as though a leopard had tried to get to the new lamb and Melech had fought him off with his big horns. Rina was afraid he might die. She loved him. She remembered how she rode on his back when she was very little, and she remembered the feel of his soft, thick wool.

Rina told Rebecca to wait with Melech and she ran to get Ephraim, the shepherd. First she went to his tent. He wasn't there. Someone said to try at the stream—maybe he went to get water. The people at the stream said that he had already left and had gone to free a ram caught by his horns in a bush. Rina ran to all the places where she thought he might be, but she couldn't find him. She was afraid that Melech would die.

Crowds of people were now walking toward the area in front of Moses' tent and she asked person after person if they had seen Ephraim. Finally someone said that he had walked on ahead, so Rina ran as fast as she could until she finally caught up to him.

Ephraim told her there wasn't a minute to lose. They ran to his tent to get medicine and bandages and then ran to Melech. Rina thanked God that Melech was still alive. Immediately Ephraim began to work. He cleaned out the wounds and bandaged the ram. Rina told Rebecca to tell her parents to go hear Moses without her. She said that she would stay and help Ephraim.

Rina was disappointed about not getting to hear Moses, but she loved Melech so much that she could not leave. All night long Rina and Ephraim took care of Melech. By the morning, Melech had stopped moaning; he opened his big eyes and licked Rina's hand. Ephraim said that it looked like he would be fine, and they could go home. Rina gave Melech a kiss, promised him she would be back later, and went home.

When she got to her tent, no one was there. In fact no one was in any of the tents. She kept walking and soon she came to the area in front of Moses' tent and she saw all the people. Everyone cheered as she came in. She was so surprised, she didn't know what to say. Then Moses spoke: "You look surprised that we are still here. We waited for you. You may think you are only a young girl, but every single one of the people is important. I know that you helped save the ram's life. You see, all of us, children and adults, must follow Torah and take care of God's world." Then Moses pointed: "See those people there?" One was on crutches, one was old and walked with a cane, and another was sitting in a cart. Moses said, "We waited for all of them too—young or old, healthy or sick, rich or poor, everyone is important. God cares about all of us. God's teachings belong to us all and each of us is part of the people of Israel."

That is all that Moses said. That is all Moses had to say. Rina and the people understood.

Values

When the Torah says, "You are all gathered before God," it means not only those in the time of Moses, but us too. Every person is important. Think about your family and your friends. Each one of you is important to them.

Every person is an essential part of the community. Everyone has a great deal to contribute, and all have a great deal they can receive back from the community.

Questions to Discuss

Why did Moses wait for Rina?

Why do you think everyone was important?

How can each person be an important part of the community?

Story-Telling Props and Tips

- a stuffed doll lamb
- bandages
- bowl for water
- crutches

46

ONE BLESSING
DOESN'T FIT ALL

HA'AZINU-V'ZOT HABRACHAH, Deuteronomy 32:1—34:12

In these final passages of the Five Books of Moses, God guides the people as a whole and blesses each individual tribe with its own blessing. This story tells how the tribes learned that the best blessing is the blessing just for them.

Adonai alone did guide (the people of Israel)...to feast on the yield of the earth. (Deuteronomy 32:12,13)

This is the blessing with which Moses, the man of God, blessed the Israelites before he died...May Reuben...And of Levi he said...Of Benjamin...And of Joseph...And of Zebulun... (Deuteronomy 33:1-25)

Shimona was still a little girl when she heard Moses bless the people. Moses was very old then and Joshua had already begun to take over most of the day-to-day tasks of leading the people. Still, Moses was their leader, and when he spoke, everyone listened. He reminded the entire people of all the blessings God had given to their people—how God had gathered them together as one people and brought them out of Egypt, led them all through the wilderness, and provided everyone with food and water.

The next day Moses was to give another speech, and Shimona wanted to be there along with all the people from her tribe. She heard that

Moses was now going to bless each tribe separately, and she was very anxious to hear what blessing her tribe would receive.

When the leaders of the tribes heard that Moses was now going to bless each tribe separately, each one claimed that his tribe should get the best blessing.

One leader said that his tribe had been great warriors in the wilderness and so they should get the best blessing. Moses told him that his tribe would receive the best blessing.

The leader of another tribe said that they had brought the most wealth out of Egypt, so they should get the best blessing. Moses told him that his tribe would get the best blessing.

The leader of still another tribe reminded Moses that his tribe had carried the ark with the commandments from Mount Sinai. He thought that they had the right to the best blessing. And again Moses told him that his tribe would have the best blessing.

Moses listened patiently to the leader of each tribe and assured them all that their tribe would get the best blessing. Each one went away happy. But as soon as they started to brag to one another about how Moses would give their tribe the best blessing, and heard that he had made the same promise to each of them, they all went back to Moses and demanded an explanation. Each one wanted to be reassured that he, and not the others, would get the best blessing.

Moses patiently assured them all that each tribe would get the best blessing. They demanded to know how they all could get the very best blessing. He promised them that he was telling the truth and they would have to wait and see. They went away grumbling and mumbling.

The next day Shimona went and stood next to the people of her tribe—Judah. This time, instead of hearing Moses say blessings of thankfulness for what they all had received as a people, she heard him ask God to be good to each of the tribes. What was special was that the wording of Moses' blessing was slightly different for each tribe.

Moses prayed that God would protect Judah from its enemies, that Levi would be a good teacher of the people, that Benjamin would be safe, that Issachar and Zebulun would be good fishermen, that Asher would have plentiful olive oil and would mine brass and iron . . . and so on. Each of the tribes receved its own special blessing. So each finally understood that they had gotten the best blessing for their own tribe.

Shimona asked her mother why each tribe had to receive a special blessing. "Aren't we all part of one people? Wouldn't it make sense to just say one blessing for us all? Wouldn't that avoid all the arguing among the tribes?"

160

Her mother answered, "Moses first reminded the people of the blessings they had all received. Now he wanted to point out what was special about each tribe. There wouldn't be any point in asking God to bless a tribe that was inland with a wealth of fish, or a tribe on rich farmland with iron and copper and brass. There wouldn't be much point in asking God to bless a tribe from the mountains with a good wheat harvest. What we ask of God has to be realistic." Her mother said, "Each of the tribes is needed for its special qualities. They are not all the same, and they each need to be recognized for what is special to them."

Then she added, "There are many blessings that our family as a whole enjoys. You and your brother and sister all are part of our family and yet each of you is different; each of you has different talents and abilities and each of you wants and needs different things. It's a little like the clothes you wear—each of you wears a different size and likes different colors. That is why we try to provide each of you with what you need and want rather than the same thing for everyone. Moses wanted to ask God to provide each of the tribes with what they needed."

Values

Each of us has different interests, needs, and special qualities, so it is important to ask God for what we need rather than looking at what others might have or want.

Questions to Discuss

Are you the same as anyone else?

Do you and your brothers and sisters or friends all like the same thing?

What blessing do you think would be best for you and your family?

Story-Telling Props and Tips

- a sword for Judah
- a book for Levi
- a fishing rod or net for Zebulun
- olive oil for Asher

GLOSSARY

Abram
The father of the Jewish people. His name was later changed to Abraham. He was the husband of Sarah and the father of Isaac and Ishmael.

Hamotzi
The name of the blessing said before eating bread.

Kiddush
A prayer, usually recited over wine, which is said on the Sabbath and festivals.

Kippah
A skullcap worn by many Jewish men and occasionally women as a sign of respect to God. Some people wear it only during prayer and study, or while eating, and others wear it all the time.

Lulav
A palm branch, which is one of the four species of plants combined and waved on the festival of Sukkot* as an expression of thankfulness to God and as a sign that God's blessings come from all directions.

Matzah
The flat, unleavened bread eaten during Passover.

Midrash
A type of Jewish literature devoted to interpretation of the biblical text. *Midrash* comes from the Hebrew word *darash*, meaning "to investigate" or "to search."

Mitzvah
Literally "commandment" given by God.

Pesah
Passover

Rosh Hashanah
The Jewish New Year, which usually occurs in September.

Sarai
The mother of the Jewish people. Her name was later changed to Sarah. Her husband was Abram* (Abraham) and her son was Isaac.

---

* See term elsewhere in this glossary.

Shabbat

The Sabbath which Jews celebrate on the seventh day. It begins on Friday evening and ends Saturday after sunset.

Shavuot

The Feast of Weeks. It receives its name because it comes seven weeks after Passover. It celebrates the late spring harvest and the giving of the Torah* at Mt. Sinai.

Shofar

A ram's horn blown on Rosh Hashanah* and Yom Kippur.* It is a call to repentance.

Sidra

The Torah* is divided into sections several chapters long. One section is read each week so that the entire Five Books of Moses is read over the course of a year.

Sukkot

The Feast of Booths. This festival begins five days after Yom Kippur* and recalls the fall harvest. During Sukkot it is customary to spend time in a booth or small temporary structure called a Sukkah, because the Jewish people used to live in them during the harvest. They also remind us of the wandering in the wilderness after the Exodus.

Tabernacle

The term frequently used for the Tent of Meeting or portable sanctuary in which the Israelites worshiped while wandering in the wilderness.

Tallit

The prayer shawl with knotted fringes called tzitzit at the corners. It is worn during morning services.

Torah

The Five Books of Moses. The Torah, which is kept in the Holy Ark in the synagogue, is a scroll written by hand on parchment.

Tzedakah

It is often translated "charity," but it is much more. Tzedakah comes from the Hebrew meaning righteousness and justice. Thus, tzedakah is the obligation to perform an act of justice. It usually refers to sharing what we have with the poor.

Yom Kippur

The Day of Atonement. It occurs ten days after Rosh Hashanah.* Jewish people fast as a sign of remorse before God for the sins they have committed during the past year.

VALUES INDEX